Simple Suppers

Copyright © 2008 Flame Tree Publishing
Flame Tree is part of The Foundry Creative Media Company Limited

This 2007 edition published by Metro Books, by arrangement with
The Foundry Creative Media Company Limited

Publisher & Creative Director: Nick Wells
Project Editor: Sarah Goulding
Designer: Mike Spender
With thanks to: Theresa Bebbington and Gina Steer

Metro Books
122 Fifth Avenue
New York, NY 10011

ISBN 13: 978-0-7607-8681-9
ISBN 10: 0-7607-8681-X

A copy of the CIP data for this book is available from the British Library.

Printed and bound in China

3 5 7 9 10 8 6 4 2

Simple Suppers

Quick and Easy Recipes

General Editor: Gina Steer

METRO BOOKS
NEW YORK

Contents

Contents

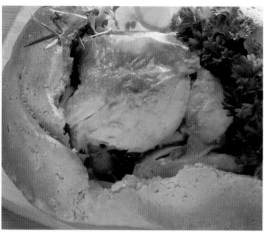

Vegetarian   **208**

Contents

Dinner Parties & Entertaining 270

Desserts 348

Hygiene in the Kitchen

It is well worth remembering that many foods can carry some form of bacteria. In most cases, the worst it will lead to is a bout of food poisoning or gastroenteritis, although for certain people this can be more serious. The risk can be reduced or eliminated by good food hygiene and proper cooking.

Do not buy or use food that is past its expiry date. When buying fresh produce or meats, use your eyes and nose. If the food looks tired, limp, or has a bad color, or if it has a rank, acrid, or simply bad smell, do not buy or eat it under any circumstances.

Always be careful when preparing raw meat and fish. A separate cutting board should be used for each; wash the knife, board, and the hands thoroughly before handling or preparing any other food.

Regularly clean, defrost, and clear out the refrigerator or freezer—it is worth checking the packaging to see exactly how long each product is safe to freeze.

Avoid handling food if you have an upset stomach, because bacteria can be passed through food preparation.

Dish cloths and kitchen towels must be washed and changed regularly. Ideally, use disposable cloths, which should be replaced on a daily basis. More durable cloths should be left to soak in bleach, then washed in the washing machine on a hot wash.

Keep your hands, cooking utensils, and food preparation surfaces clean, and do not allow pets to climb onto any work surfaces.

Buying

Avoid bulk buying where possible, especially fresh produce, such as meat, poultry, fish, and fruit and vegetables, unless you are buying them for the freezer. Fresh foods lose their nutritional value rapidly, so buying a little at a time minimizes the loss of nutrients. It also avoids a packed refrigerator, which reduces the effectiveness of the refrigeration process.

When buying prepackaged goods, such as cans or containers of beans or yogurt, check that the packaging is intact and not damaged or pierced at all. Cans should not be dented, pierced, or rusty. Check the expiry dates for cans and packages of dry ingredients, such as flour and rice. Store fresh foods in the refrigerator as soon as possible—not in the car or the office.

When buying frozen foods, ensure that they are not heavily iced on the outside and the contents are completely frozen. Make sure the frozen foods have been stored at the correct storage level and the temperature is below -0.4°F. Pack them in insulated bags to transport home and place in the freezer as soon as possible after purchase.

Preparation

Make sure that all work surfaces and utensils are clean and dry. Hygiene should be given priority at all times. Separate cutting boards should be used for raw and cooked meats, fish, and vegetables. Currently, a variety of good-quality plastic boards come in various designs and colors. This makes differentiating easier and the plastic has the added hygienic advantage of being washable at high temperatures in the dishwasher. (Note: If using the board for fish, first wash in cold water, then in hot to prevent it from retaining an odor!) Also, remember that knives and utensils should always be thoroughly cleaned after use.

When cooking, be particularly careful to keep cooked and raw food separate to avoid any contamination. It is worth washing all fruit and vegetables regardless of whether they will be eaten raw or lightly cooked. This rule should apply even to prewashed herbs and salads.

Do not reheat food more than once. If using a microwave, always check that the food is piping hot all the way through. In theory, the food should reach 158°F and needs to be cooked at that temperature for at least three minutes to ensure that all bacteria are killed.

All poultry must be thoroughly thawed before using, including chicken and poussin. Remove the food to be thawed from the freezer and place in a shallow dish to contain the juices. Let the food stand in the refrigerator until it is completely thawed. A 3 lb whole chicken will take about 26–30 hours to thaw. To speed up the process, immerse the chicken in cold water. However, make sure that the water is changed regularly. When the joints can move freely and no ice crystals remain in the cavity, the bird is completely thawed.

Once thawed, remove its wrapper and pat the chicken dry. Place the chicken in a shallow dish, cover lightly, and store as close to the bottom of the refrigerator as possible. The chicken should be cooked as soon as possible.

Some foods can be cooked from frozen, including many prepackaged foods, such as soups, sauces, casseroles, and breads. Where applicable follow the manufacturers' instructions.

Vegetables and fruit can also be cooked from frozen, but meats and fish should be thawed first. The only time food can be refrozen is when the food has been thoroughly thawed then

cooked. Once the food has cooled then it can be frozen again. On such occasions the food can only be stored for one month.

All poultry and game (except for duck) must be cooked thoroughly. When cooked the juices will run clear from the thickest part of the bird—the best area to try is usually the thigh. Other meats, such as ground beef and pork, should be cooked all the way through. Fish should turn opaque, be firm in texture, and break easily into large flakes.

When cooking leftovers, make sure they are reheated until piping hot and that any sauce or soup reaches boiling point first.

Storing, Refrigerating & Freezing

Meat, poultry, fish, seafood, and dairy products should all be refrigerated. The temperature of the refrigerator should be between 34–41°F, while the freezer temperature should not rise above -0.4°F.

To ensure the optimum refrigerator and freezer temperature, avoid leaving the door open for a long time. Avoid overstocking the refrigerator because this reduces the airflow inside and affects the effectiveness in cooling the food within.

When refrigerating cooked food, let it cool down quickly and completely before refrigerating. Hot food will raise the temperature of the refrigerator and possibly affect or spoil other food stored in it.

Food within the refrigerator and freezer should always be covered. Raw and cooked food should be stored in separate parts of the refrigerator. Cooked food should be kept on the top shelves of the refrigerator, while raw meat, poultry, and

fish should be placed on bottom shelves to avoid drips and cross-contamination. It is recommended that eggs should be refrigerated in order to maintain their freshness and shelf life.

Be careful that frozen foods are not stored in the freezer for too long. Blanched vegetables can be stored for one month; beef, lamb, poultry, and pork for six months; and unblanched vegetables and fruit in syrup for a year. Oily fish and sausages can be stored for three months. Dairy products can last four to six months, while cakes and pastries can be kept in the freezer for three to six months.

High-Risk Foods

Certain foods may carry risks to people who are considered vulnerable such as the elderly, the ill, pregnant women, babies, young infants, and those suffering from a recurring illness.

It is advisable that these people avoid the foods listed below, which belong to a higher-risk category.

There is a slight chance that some eggs carry the bacteria salmonella. Cook the eggs until both the yolk and the white are firm to eliminate this risk. Pay particular attention to dishes and products incorporating lightly cooked or raw eggs, which should be eliminated from the diet. Sauces, including Hollandaise, mayonnaise, mousses, soufflés, and meringues, all use raw or lightly cooked eggs, as do custard-based dishes, ice creams, and sorbets. These are all considered high-risk foods to the vulnerable groups mentioned above.

Certain meats and poultry also carry the potential risk of salmonella and so should be cooked thoroughly until the juices run clear and there is no pinkness left. Unpasteurized products, such as milk, cheese (especially soft cheese), pâté, and meat (both raw and cooked) all have the potential risk of listeria and should be avoided.

When buying seafood, buy from a reputable source that has a high turnover to ensure freshness. Fish should have bright clear eyes, shiny skin, and bright pink or red gills. The fish should feel stiff to the touch, and there should be a slight smell of sea air and iodine. The flesh of fish steaks and fillets should be translucent with no signs of discoloration.

Mollusks, such as scallops, clams, and mussels, are sold fresh and are still alive. Avoid any that are open or do not close when tapped lightly. In the same way, univalves, such as periwinkles, should withdraw back into their shells when lightly prodded. When choosing cephalopods, such as squid and octopus, remember they should have a firm flesh and pleasant sea smell.

As with all fish, whether it is shellfish or seafish, care is required when freezing it. It is imperative to check whether the fish has been frozen before. If it has been frozen, then it should not be frozen again under any circumstances.

Herbs & Spices

The use of herbs and spices can make all the difference between a bland and a tasty dish. Some of the most common herbs and spices, along with their uses, are listed below.

ALLSPICE The dark allspice berries come whole or ground and have a flavor similar to that of cinnamon, cloves, and nutmeg.

BASIL Best fresh but also available in dried form, basil can be used raw or cooked and works particularly well in tomato-based and Mediterranean dishes.

BAY LEAVES Are available in fresh or dried form as well as ground. They make up part of a bouquet garni and are particularly delicious when added to meat and poultry dishes, soups, stews, vegetable dishes, and stuffing. They also impart a spicy flavor to milk puddings and custards.

BOUQUET GARNI is a bouquet of fresh herbs tied with a piece of string or in a small piece of muslin. It is used to flavor casseroles, stews, stocks, and sauces. The herbs that are normally used are parsley, thyme, and bay leaves.

CAYENNE This powdered form of a red chile pepper is said to be native to Cayenne. It is similar in appearance to paprika and can be used sparingly to add a fiery kick to many dishes.

CARDAMOM Cardamom has a distinctive, sweet, rich taste and can be bought whole in the pod, in seed form, or ground. This sweet aromatic spice is delicious in rice, cakes, and cookies and is great served with rice pudding and fruit.

CHERVIL Reminiscent of parsley and available either in fresh or dried form, chervil has a faintly sweet spicy flavor and is particularly good in soups, cheese dishes, stews, and with eggs.

CHILE Available whole, fresh, dried, and in powdered form, red chile peppers tend to be sweeter in taste than their green counterparts. They are particularly associated with Spanish and Mexican-style cooking and Indian dishes.

CHIVES This member of the onion family is ideal for use when a delicate onion flavor is required. Chives are good with eggs, cheese, fish, and vegetable dishes. They also work well as a garnish for soups, meat, and vegetable dishes.

CILANTRO The leaves of the same plant that provides coriander seeds are used to flavor spicy aromatic dishes as well as being used as a garnish.

CLOVES Mainly used whole but available ground, cloves have a warm, sweet pungent aroma and can be used to stud roast ham and pork, in mulled wine and punch, and to pickle fruit.

CORIANDER These seeds have an orangey flavor and are delicious in casseroles, Indian dishes, and for pickling.

CUMIN Also available ground or as whole seeds, cumin has a strong, slightly bitter flavor. It is one of the main ingredients in curry powder and compliments fish, meat, and rice dishes.

GINGER Ginger comes in many forms but primarily as a fresh root and in dried ground form, which can be used in baking, Indian dishes, pickles, sauces, and Chinese cooking.

LEMON GRASS Available fresh and dried, with a subtle, aromatic, lemony flavor, lemon grass is essential to Thai cooking. It is also delicious when added to soups, poultry, and fish dishes.

MARJORAM Often dried, marjoram has a sweet slightly spicy flavor, which tastes fantastic when added to stuffing, meat, or tomato-based dishes.

OREGANO The strongly flavored dried leaves are similar to marjoram and are used extensively in Italian and Greek cooking.

PAPRIKA Paprika often comes in two varieties. One is sweet and mild and the other has a slight bite to it. Paprika is made from the fruit of the bell pepper and is good in meat and poultry dishes, as well as a garnish. The rule of buying herbs and spices little and often applies particularly to paprika as unfortunately it does not keep particularly well.

PARSLEY The stems as well as the leaves of parsley can be used to compliment most savory dishes as they contain the most flavor. They can also be used as a garnish.

PEPPER This comes in white and black peppercorns and is best freshly ground. Both add flavor to most dishes, sauces, and gravies. Black pepper has a more robust flavor, while white pepper has a much more delicate flavor.

ROSEMARY The small needlelike leaves have a sweet aroma, which is particularly good with lamb, stuffing, and vegetable dishes.

SAFFRON Deep orange in color, saffron is traditionally used in paella, rice, and cakes, but is also delicious with poultry.

SAGE The fresh or dried leaves have a pungent, slightly bitter taste, which is delicious with pork and poultry, sausages, stuffing, and with stuffed pasta when tossed in a little butter and fresh sage.

SAVORY This herb resembles thyme, but has a softer flavor that particularly complements all types of fish and beans.

TARRAGON The fresh or dried leaves of tarragon have a sweet aromatic taste, which is particularly good with poultry, seafood, and fish.

THYME Available fresh or dried, thyme has a pungent flavor and is included in bouquet garni. It complements many meat and poultry dishes and stuffing.

TURMERIC This root is ground and has a brilliant yellow color. It has a bitter peppery flavor and is often used in curry powder and mustard.

Light Bites

Quick Mediterranean Shrimp

SERVES 4

20 raw Mediterranean shrimp
3 tbsp olive oil
1 garlic clove, peeled and crushed
finely grated zest and juice of ½ lemon

sprigs of fresh rosemary

For the pesto & sun-dried tomato dips:
⅔ cup whole-milk plain yogurt
1 tbsp prepared pesto

⅔ cup crème fraîche or sour cream
1 tbsp sun-dried tomato paste
1 tbsp whole-grain mustard
salt and freshly ground black pepper
lemon wedges, to garnish

Remove the shells from the shrimp, leaving the tail shells. Using a small, sharp knife, remove the dark vein that runs along the back of the shrimp. Rinse and drain on a paper towel.

Whisk 2 tablespoons of the oil with the garlic and lemon zest and juice in a small bowl. Bruise 1 sprig of rosemary with a rolling pin and add to the bowl. Add the shrimp, toss to coat, then cover and let marinate in the refrigerator until needed.

For the simple dips, mix the yogurt and pesto in one bowl and the crème fraîche, tomato paste, and mustard in another bowl. Season to taste with salt and pepper.

Heat a wok, add the remaining oil, and swirl round to coat the sides. Remove the shrimp from the marinade, leaving any juices and the rosemary behind. Add to the wok and stir-fry over a high heat for 3–4 minutes, or until the shrimp are pink and just cooked through.

Remove the shrimp from the wok and arrange on a platter. Garnish with lemon wedges and more fresh rosemary sprigs, and serve hot or cold with the dips.

Try this: FOR MAIN MEAL: 68   FOR DESSERT: 352

Thai Fish Cakes

SERVES 4

1 red chile pepper, deseeded and roughly chopped
4 tbsp roughly chopped fresh cilantro
1 garlic clove, peeled and crushed
2 green onions, trimmed and roughly chopped
1 lemon grass, outer leaves discarded and roughly chopped
3 oz shrimp, thawed if frozen
10 oz cod fillet, skinned, bones removed, and cubed
salt and freshly ground black pepper
sweet chili pepper dipping sauce, to serve

Preheat the oven to 375°F. Place the chile pepper, cilantro, garlic, green onions, and lemon grass in a food processor and blend together.

Pat the shrimp and cod dry with a paper towel.

Add to the food processor and blend until the mixture is roughly chopped.

Season to taste with salt and pepper and blend to mix.

Dampen your hands, then shape heaped tablespoons of the mixture into 12 little patties.

Place the patties on a lightly oiled baking sheet and cook in the preheated oven for 12–15 minutes, or until piping hot and cooked through. Turn the patties over halfway through the cooking time.

Serve the fish cakes immediately with the sweet chili sauce for dipping.

Try this: FOR MAIN MEAL: 86   FOR DESSERT: 362

Fried Smelt with Arugula Salad

SERVES 4

1 lb smelt, fresh
  or frozen
oil, for frying
¾ cup all-purpose flour
½ tsp of cayenne pepper
salt and freshly ground
  black pepper

For the salad:
4 cups arugula
8 cherry tomatoes,
  halved
½ medium cucumber,
  diced
3 tbsp olive oil

1 tbsp fresh lemon juice
½ tsp Dijon mustard
½ tsp superfine sugar

If the smelt are frozen, thaw completely, then wipe dry with a paper towel.

Start to heat the oil in a deep-fat fryer. Arrange the fish in a large, shallow dish and toss well in the flour, cayenne pepper, and salt and pepper.

Deep-fry the fish in batches for 2–3 minutes, or until crisp and golden. Keep the cooked fish warm while deep-frying the remaining fish.

Meanwhile, to make the salad, arrange the arugula, cherry tomatoes, and cucumber on individual serving dishes. Whisk the olive oil and the remaining ingredients together and season lightly. Drizzle the dressing over the salad and serve with the smelt.

Try this: FOR MAIN MEAL: 186   FOR DESSERT: 364

Hot Shrimp
with Parma Ham

SERVES 4

½ cucumber,
   peeled if preferred
4 ripe tomatoes
12 large, raw shrimp
6 tbsp olive oil

4 garlic cloves,
   peeled and crushed
4 tbsp freshly chopped
   parsley
salt and freshly ground

black pepper
6 slices of Parma ham or
   prosciutto, cut in half
4 slices flat Italian bread
4 tbsp dry white wine

Preheat oven to 350°F. Slice the cucumber and tomatoes thinly, then arrange on 4 large plates and reserve. Peel the shrimp, leaving the tail shell intact, and remove the thin black vein running down the back.

Whisk together 4 tablespoons of the olive oil, garlic, and chopped parsley in a small bowl, and season to taste with plenty of salt and pepper. Add the shrimp to the mixture and stir until they are well coated. Remove the shrimp, then wrap each one in a piece of Parma ham and secure with a toothpick.

Place the prepared shrimp on a lightly oiled baking sheet or dish with the slices of bread and cook in the preheated oven for 5 minutes.

Remove the shrimp from the oven and spoon the wine over the shrimp and bread. Return to the oven and cook for a further 10 minutes, until piping hot.

Carefully remove the toothpicks and arrange three shrimp rolls on each slice of bread. Place on top of the sliced cucumber and tomatoes and serve immediately.

Try this: FOR MAIN MEAL: 114   FOR DESSERT: 358

Warm Swordfish Niçoise

SERVES 4

4 swordfish steaks (about
  6 oz each), 1 inch thick
juice of 1 lime
2 tbsp olive oil
salt and freshly ground
  black pepper
14 oz farfalle

1¾ cups green beans, topped
  and cut in half
1 tsp Dijon mustard
2 tsp white wine vinegar
pinch superfine sugar
3 tbsp olive oil
2 medium tomatoes,

  quartered
8 large, pitted black olives
2 medium eggs, hard boiled
  and quartered
8 anchovy fillets, drained
  and cut in half lengthways

Place the swordfish steaks in a shallow dish. Mix the lime juice with the oil, season to taste with salt and pepper, and spoon over the steaks. Turn the steaks to coat them evenly. Cover and place them in the refrigerator to marinate for 1 hour.

Bring a large saucepan of lightly salted water to a rapid boil. Add the farfalle and cook according to the package instructions, or until cooked but still firm. Add the green beans about 4 minutes before the end of cooking time.

Mix the mustard, vinegar, and sugar together in a small jug. Gradually whisk in the olive oil to make a thick dressing. Cook the swordfish in a griddle pan or under a hot preheated broiler for 2 minutes on each side, or until just cooked through; overcooking will make it tough and dry. Remove and cut into ¾-inch chunks.

Drain the pasta and beans thoroughly and place in a large bowl. Pour over the dressing and toss to coat. Add the cooked swordfish, tomatoes, olives, hard-boiled eggs, and anchovy fillets. Gently toss together, taking care not to break up the eggs.

Tip into a warmed serving bowl or divide the pasta between individual plates. Serve immediately.

Try this: FOR MAIN MEAL: 72 FOR DESSERT: 372

Mixed Salad with Anchovy Dressing & Ciabatta Croutons

SERVES 4

1 small head endive
1 small head chicory
1 fennel bulb
14-oz can artichokes,
    drained and rinsed
½ cucumber
8 cherry tomatoes
12 large black olives

For the anchovy dressing:
1¾-oz can anchovy fillets
1 tsp Dijon mustard
1 small garlic clove, peeled
    and crushed
4 tbsp olive oil
1 tbsp lemon juice
freshly ground black pepper

For the ciabatta croutons:
2 thick slices ciabatta bread
2 tbsp olive oil

Divide the endive and chicory into leaves and reserve some of the larger ones. Arrange the smaller leaves in a wide salad bowl.

Cut the fennel bulb in half from the stalk to the root end, then cut across in fine slices. Quarter the artichokes, then quarter and slice the cucumber and halve the tomatoes. Add to the salad bowl with the olives.

To make the dressing, drain the anchovies and put in a blender with the mustard, garlic, olive oil, lemon juice, 2 tablespoons of hot water, and black pepper. Whiz together until smooth and thickened.

To make the croutons, cut the bread into ½-inch cubes. Heat the oil in a skillet, add the bread cubes, and fry for 3 minutes, turning frequently until golden. Remove and drain on a paper towel.

Drizzle half the anchovy dressing over the prepared salad and toss to coat. Arrange the reserved endive and chicory leaves around the edge, then drizzle over the remaining dressing. Scatter over the croutons and serve immediately.

Try this: FOR MAIN MEAL: 120   FOR DESSERT: 350

Crispy Shrimp with Chinese Dipping Sauce

SERVES 4

1 lb medium-sized
   raw shrimp, peeled
¼ tsp salt
6 tbsp peanut oil
2 garlic cloves, peeled
   and finely chopped
1 inch piece fresh ginger,
   peeled and finely chopped

1 green chile pepper,
   deseeded and finely
   chopped
4 stems fresh cilantro,
   leaves and stems
   roughly chopped

For the Chinese
   dipping sauce:
3 tbsp dark soy sauce
3 tbsp rice wine vinegar
1 tbsp superfine sugar
2 tbsp chile oil
2 green onions,
   finely shredded

Using a sharp knife, remove the black vein along the back of the shrimp. Sprinkle the shrimp with the salt and let stand for 15 minutes. Pat dry on a paper towel.

Heat a wok or large skillet and add the peanut oil; when hot, add the shrimp and stir-fry in 2 batches for about 1 minute, or until they turn pink and are almost cooked. Using a slotted spoon, remove the shrimp and keep warm in a low oven.

Drain the oil from the wok, leaving 1 tablespoon. Add the garlic, ginger, and chile pepper, and cook for about 30 seconds. Add the cilantro, return the shrimp, and stir-fry for 1–2 minutes, or until the shrimp are cooked through and the garlic is golden. Turn into a warmed serving dish.

For the dipping sauce, using a fork, beat together the soy sauce, rice vinegar, superfine sugar, and chile oil in a small bowl. Stir in the green onions. Serve immediately with the hot shrimp.

Fresh Tuna Salad

SERVES 4

8 cups mixed
  lettuce leaves
16 baby cherry tomatoes,
  halved lengthways
4 cups arugula, washed
2 tbsp peanut oil
1¼ lb boned tuna steaks,

each cut into
  4 small pieces

2-oz piece fresh
  Parmesan cheese

For the dressing:
8 tbsp olive oil
grated zest and juice of
  2 small lemons
1 tbsp whole-grain mustard
salt and freshly ground
  black pepper

Wash the lettuce, place in a large bowl with the cherry tomatoes and arugula, and reserve.

Heat the wok, then add the oil and heat until almost smoking. Add the tuna, skin-side down, and cook for 4–6 minutes, turning once during cooking, or until cooked and the flesh flakes easily. Remove from the heat and let stand in the juices for 2 minutes before removing.

Meanwhile make the dressing: Place the olive oil, lemon zest and juice, and mustard in a small bowl or screw-topped jar and whisk or shake well until well blended. Season to taste with salt and pepper.

Transfer the tuna to a clean cutting board and flake, then add it to the salad and toss lightly.

Using a swivel-blade vegetable peeler, peel the piece of Parmesan cheese into shavings. Divide the salad between four large serving plates, drizzle the dressing over the salad, then scatter with the Parmesan shavings.

Try this: FOR MAIN MEAL: 88   FOR DESSERT: 368

Sweet & Sour Spare Ribs

SERVES 4

3½ lb pork spare ribs
4 tbsp clear honey
1 tbsp Worcestershire sauce
1 tsp Chinese five spice
   powder

4 tbsp soy sauce
2½ tbsp dry sherry
1 tsp chili sauce
2 garlic cloves, peeled
   and chopped

1½ tbsp tomato paste
1 tsp dry mustard powder
   (optional)
green onion curls,
   to garnish

Preheat the oven to 400°F, 15 minutes before cooking. If necessary, place the ribs on a cutting board and using a sharp knife, cut the joint in between the ribs to form single ribs. Place the ribs in a shallow dish in a single layer.

Add the honey, Worcestershire sauce, and Chinese five spice powder with the soy sauce, sherry, and chili sauce to a small saucepan and heat gently, stirring until smooth. Stir in the chopped garlic, the tomato paste, and mustard powder, if using.

Pour the honey mixture over the ribs and spoon over until the ribs are coated evenly. Cover with plastic wrap and let marinate overnight in the refrigerator, occasionally spooning the marinade over the ribs.

When ready to cook, remove the ribs from the marinade and place in a shallow roasting pan. Spoon over a little of the marinade and reserve the remainder. Place the spare ribs in the preheated oven and cook for 35–40 minutes, or until cooked and the outsides are crisp. Baste occasionally with the reserved marinade during cooking. Garnish with a few green onion curls and serve immediately, either as a starter or as a meat accompaniment.

Chinese Cabbage & Mushroom Soup

SERVES 4-6

1 lb Chinese cabbage
6 dried shiitake mushrooms
1 tbsp vegetable oil
3 oz smoked bacon, diced
1-inch piece fresh ginger,
    peeled and finely chopped
2½ cups button mushrooms,
    thinly sliced
4½ cups chicken stock
4–6 green onions, trimmed
    and cut into short lengths
2 tbsp dry sherry or
    Chinese rice wine
salt and freshly ground
black pepper
sesame oil for drizzling

Trim the stem ends of the Chinese cabbage and cut in half lengthways. Remove the triangular core with a knife, then cut into 1-inch slices and reserve.

Place the dried shiitake mushrooms in a bowl and pour over enough almost boiling water to cover. Let stand for 20 minutes to soften, then gently lift out and squeeze out the liquid. Discard the stems and thinly slice the caps and reserve. Strain the liquid through a muslin-lined sieve or a paper coffee filter and reserve.

Heat a wok over a medium-high heat and add the oil; when hot, add the bacon. Stir-fry for 3–4 minutes, or until crisp and golden, stirring frequently. Add the ginger and button mushrooms and stir-fry for a further 2–3 minutes.

Add the chicken stock and bring to a boil, skimming any fat and scum that rises to the surface. Add the green onions, sherry or rice wine, Chinese cabbage, and sliced shiitake mushrooms, and season to taste with salt and pepper. Pour in the reserved soaking liquid and reduce the heat to the lowest setting.

Simmer gently, covered, until all the vegetables are tender; this will take about 10 minutes. Add a little water if the liquid has reduced too much. Spoon into soup bowls and drizzle with a little sesame oil. Serve immediately.

Try this: FOR MAIN MEAL: 104 FOR DESSERT: 356

Crispy Baked Potatoes with Serrano Ham

SERVES 4

4 large baking potatoes	2 oz lean serrano ham or	⅓ cup cooked carrots, diced
4 tsp crème fraîche or	prosciutto, with fat	⅓ cup cooked peas
sour cream	removed	½ cup hard cheese, such as
salt and freshly ground	½ cup cooked baby	Edam or Cheddar, grated
black pepper	fava beans	fresh green salad, to serve

Preheat the oven to 400°F. Scrub the potatoes dry. Prick with a fork and place on a baking sheet. Cook for 1–1½ hours or until tender when squeezed. (Use oven mitts or a kitchen towel to pick up the potatoes—they will be hot.)

Cut the potatoes in half horizontally and scoop out all the flesh into a bowl.

Spoon the crème fraîche into the bowl and mix thoroughly with the potatoes. Season to taste with a little salt and pepper.

Cut the ham into strips and carefully stir into the potato mixture with the fava beans, carrots, and peas.

Pile the mixture back into the potato shells and sprinkle a little grated cheese on the top.

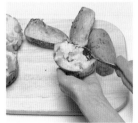

Place under a hot broiler and cook until golden and heated through. Serve immediately with a fresh green salad.

Bacon & Split Pea Soup

SERVES 4

¼ cup dried split peas
2 tbsp butter
1 garlic clove, peeled and
    finely chopped
1 medium onion, peeled and
    thinly sliced
1 cup long-grain rice

2 tbsp tomato paste
4½ cups vegetable or
    chicken stock
2 medium carrots, peeled
    and finely diced
4 oz streaky bacon,
    finely chopped

salt and freshly ground
    black pepper
2 tbsp freshly chopped
    parsley
4 tbsp light cream
warm crusty garlic bread,
    to serve

Cover the dried split peas with plenty of cold water, cover loosely, and let soak for a minimum of 12 hours, preferably overnight.

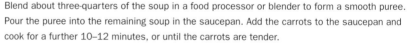

Melt the butter in a heavy-based saucepan, add the garlic and onion, and cook for 2–3 minutes, without letting them color. Add the rice, drained split peas, and tomato paste, and cook for 2–3 minutes, stirring constantly to prevent sticking. Add the stock, bring to a boil, then reduce the heat and simmer for 20–25 minutes, or until the rice and peas are tender. Remove from the heat and let cool.

Blend about three-quarters of the soup in a food processor or blender to form a smooth puree. Pour the puree into the remaining soup in the saucepan. Add the carrots to the saucepan and cook for a further 10–12 minutes, or until the carrots are tender.

Meanwhile, place the bacon in a nonstick skillet and cook over a gentle heat until the bacon is crisp. Remove and drain on a paper towel.

Season the soup with salt and pepper to taste, then stir in the parsley and cream. Reheat for 2–3 minutes, then ladle into soup bowls. Sprinkle with the bacon and serve immediately with warm garlic bread.

Try this: FOR MAIN MEAL: 70 FOR DESSERT: 378

Soy-glazed Chicken Thighs

SERVES 6-8

2 lb chicken thighs
2 tbsp vegetable oil
3–4 garlic cloves, peeled
    and crushed
1½-inch piece fresh ginger,
    peeled and finely chopped

or grated
½ cup soy sauce
2–3 tbsp Chinese rice wine
    or dry sherry
2 tbsp clear honey
1 tbsp brown sugar

2–3 dashes hot chili sauce,
    or to taste
freshly chopped parsley,
    to garnish

Heat a large wok and add the oil; when hot, stir-fry the chicken thighs for 5 minutes, or until golden. Remove and drain on a paper towel. You may need to do this in 2–3 batches.

Pour off the oil and fat and, using a paper towel, carefully wipe out the wok. Add the garlic, with the ginger, soy sauce, Chinese rice wine or sherry, and honey to the wok, and stir well. Sprinkle in the brown sugar with the hot chili sauce to taste, then place over the heat and bring to a boil.

Reduce the heat to a gentle simmer, then carefully add the chicken thighs. Cover the wok and simmer gently over a low heat for 30 minutes, or until they are tender and the sauce is reduced and thickened and glazes the chicken thighs.

Stir or spoon the sauce occasionally over the chicken thighs and add a little water if the sauce is starting to become too thick. Arrange in a shallow serving dish, garnish with freshly chopped parsley and serve immediately.

Try this: FOR MAIN MEAL: 158 FOR DESSERT: 376

Cheesy Chicken Burgers

SERVES 6

1 tbsp sunflower oil
1 small onion, peeled and finely chopped
1 garlic clove, peeled and crushed
½ red bell pepper, deseeded and finely chopped
1 lb freshly ground chicken
2 tbsp low-fat plain yogurt
1 cup fresh brown bread crumbs
1 tbsp freshly chopped

herbs, such as parsley or tarragon
½ cup Cheddar cheese, crumbled
salt and freshly ground black pepper

For the sweet corn and carrot relish:
7-oz can corn kernels, drained
1 carrot, peeled and grated

½ green chile pepper, deseeded and finely chopped
2 tsp cider vinegar
2 tsp light brown sugar

To serve:
whole-grain rolls
lettuce
sliced tomatoes

Preheat the broiler. Heat the oil in a skillet and gently cook the onion and garlic for 5 minutes. Add the red bell pepper and cook for 5 minutes. Transfer into a mixing bowl and reserve. Add the chicken, yogurt, bread crumbs, herbs, and cheese, and season to taste with salt and pepper. Mix well. Divide the mixture equally into six and shape into burgers. Cover and chill in the refrigerator for at least 20 minutes.

To make the relish, put all the ingredients in a small saucepan with 1 tablespoon of water and heat gently, stirring occasionally until all the sugar has dissolved. Cover and cook over a low heat for 2 minutes, then uncover and cook for a further minute, or until the relish is thick.

Place the burgers on a lightly oiled broiler pan and broil under a medium heat for 8–10 minutes on each side, or until browned and completely cooked through.

Warm the rolls if liked, then split in half and fill with the burgers, lettuce, sliced tomatoes and the prepared relish. Serve immediately.

Try this: FOR MAIN MEAL: 172 FOR DESSERT: 370

Chicken & Pasta Salad

SERVES 6

1 lb short pasta

2–3 tbsp extra virgin olive oil

11 oz cold cooked chicken, cut into bite-sized pieces (preferably roasted)

1 red bell pepper, deseeded and diced

1 yellow bell pepper, deseeded and diced

4–5 sun-dried tomatoes, sliced

2 tbsp capers, rinsed and drained

26 large pitted Italian black olives

4 green onions, chopped

2 cups mozzarella cheese, diced

salt and freshly ground black pepper

For the dressing:

¼ cup red or white wine vinegar

1 tbsp mild mustard

1 tsp sugar

⅓–½ cup extra virgin olive oil

½ cup mayonnaise

Bring a large saucepan of lightly salted water to a rapid boil. Add the pasta and cook for 10 minutes, or until cooked but still firm.

Drain the pasta and rinse under cold running water, then drain again. Place in a large serving bowl and toss with the olive oil.

Add the chicken, diced red and yellow bell peppers, sliced sun-dried tomatoes, capers, olives, green onions, and mozzarella to the pasta, and toss gently until mixed. Season to taste with salt and pepper.

To make the dressing, put the vinegar, mustard, and sugar into a small bowl or jug and whisk until well blended and the sugar is dissolved. Season with some pepper, then gradually whisk in the olive oil in a slow, steady stream until a thickened vinaigrette forms.

Put the mayonnaise in a bowl and gradually whisk in the dressing until smooth. Pour over the pasta mixture and mix gently until all the ingredients are coated. Turn into a large, shallow serving bowl and serve at room temperature.

Try this: FOR MAIN MEAL: 168   FOR DESSERT: 354

Oriental Noodle & Peanut Salad with Cilantro

SERVES 4

12 oz rice vermicelli
4¼ cups low-fat chicken
stock
2 tsp sesame oil
2 tbsp light soy sauce
8 green onions

3 tbsp peanut oil
2 hot green chile peppers,
deseeded and thinly
sliced
4 tbsp roughly chopped
cilantro

2 tbsp freshly chopped mint
½ medium cucumber, finely
chopped
½ cup bean sprouts
4½ tbsp roasted peanuts,
roughly chopped

Put the noodles into a large bowl. Bring the stock to a boil and immediately pour over the noodles. Let soak for 4 minutes, or according to the package directions. Drain well, discarding the stock or saving it for another use. Mix together the sesame oil and soy sauce and pour over the hot noodles. Toss well to coat and let stand until cold.

Trim and thinly slice 4 of the green onions. Heat the oil in a wok over a low heat. Add the green onions and, as soon as they sizzle, remove from the heat and let cool. When cold, toss with the noodles.

On a cutting board, cut the remaining green onions lengthways 4–6 times, and keep in a bowl of cold water until tassels form. Serve the noodles in individual bowls, each dressed with a little chile pepper, cilantro, mint, cucumber, bean sprouts, and peanuts. Garnish with the green onion tassels and serve.

Tortellini, Cherry Tomato & Mozzarella Skewers

SERVES 6

9 oz mixed green and plain
   cheese or vegetable-filled
   fresh tortellini
⅔ cup extra virgin olive oil
2 garlic cloves, peeled
   and crushed

pinch dried thyme or basil
salt and freshly ground
   black pepper
18 cherry tomatoes
1 lb mozzarella, cut into
   1-inch cubes

basil leaves, to garnish
dressed lettuce leaves,
   to serve

Preheat the broiler and line broiler grill pan with foil just before cooking. Bring a large saucepan of lightly salted water to a rapid boil. Add the tortellini and cook according to the package instructions, or until cooked but still firm. Drain, rinse under cold running water, drain again, and toss with 2 tablespoons of the olive oil and reserve.

Pour the remaining olive oil into a small bowl. Add the crushed garlic and thyme or basil, then blend well. Season to taste with salt and black pepper and reserve.

To assemble the skewers, thread the tortellini alternately with the cherry tomatoes and cubes of mozzarella. Arrange the skewers on the broiler pan and brush generously on all sides with the olive oil mixture.

Cook the skewers under the preheated broiler for about 5 minutes, or until they begin to turn golden, turning them halfway through cooking. Arrange two skewers on each plate and garnish with a few basil leaves. Serve immediately with dressed lettuce leaves.

Try this: FOR MAIN MEAL: 134   FOR DESSERT: 372

Panzanella

SERVES 4

12 slices day-old, Italian-
   style bread
1 tbsp red wine vinegar
4 tbsp olive oil
1 tsp lemon juice
1 small garlic clove, peeled
   and finely chopped

1 red onion, peeled
   and finely sliced
1 cucumber, peeled
   if preferred
2 medium tomatoes,
   deseeded
30 large, pitted black olives

about 20 basil leaves,
   coarsely torn or left
   whole if small
sea salt and freshly ground
   black pepper

Cut the bread into thick slices, leaving the crusts on. Add 1 teaspoon of red wine vinegar to a jug of iced water, put the slices of bread in a bowl, and pour over the water. Make sure the bread is covered completely. Let soak for 3–4 minutes, until just soft.

Remove the soaked bread from the water and squeeze it gently, first with your hands and then in a clean kitchen towel, to remove any excess water. Put the bread on a plate, cover with plastic wrap, and chill in the refrigerator for about 1 hour.

Meanwhile, whisk together the olive oil, the remaining red wine vinegar, and lemon juice in a large serving bowl. Add the garlic and onion and stir to coat well.

Halve the cucumber and remove the seeds. Chop both the cucumber and tomatoes into ½-inch dice. Add to the garlic and onions with the olives. Tear the bread into bite-sized chunks and add to the bowl with the fresh basil leaves. Toss together to mix and serve immediately, with a grinding of sea salt and black pepper.

Try this: FOR MAIN MEAL: 176 FOR DESSERT: 356

Mozzarella Frittata
with Tomato & Basil Salad

SERVES 6

For the salad:
6 ripe but firm tomatoes
2 tbsp fresh basil leaves
2 tbsp olive oil
1 tbsp fresh lemon juice
1 tsp superfine sugar
freshly ground black pepper

For the frittata:
7 medium eggs, beaten
salt
3 cups mozzarella cheese
2 green onions, trimmed
   and finely chopped
2 tbsp olive oil

warm crusty bread,
   to serve

To make the tomato and basil salad, slice the tomatoes thinly, tear up the basil leaves, and sprinkle over. Make the dressing by whisking the olive oil, lemon juice, and sugar together well. Season with black pepper before drizzling the dressing over the salad.

To make the frittata, preheat the broiler to a high heat just before beginning to cook. Place the eggs in a large bowl with plenty of salt and whisk. Grate the mozzarella and stir into the egg with the finely chopped green onions.

Heat the oil in a large, nonstick skillet and pour in the egg mixture, stirring with a wooden spoon to spread the ingredients evenly over the pan.

Cook for 5–8 minutes, until the frittata is golden brown and firm on the underside. Place the whole pan under the preheated broiler and cook for about 4–5 minutes, or until the top is golden brown. Slide the frittata onto a serving plate, cut into six large wedges, and serve immediately with the tomato and basil salad and plenty of warm crusty bread.

Bread & Tomato Soup

SERVES 4

7 medium tomatoes
   (about 2 lb)
4 tbsp olive oil
1 onion, peeled and
   finely chopped
1 tbsp freshly chopped basil

3 garlic cloves, peeled
   and crushed
¼ tsp hot chili powder
salt and freshly ground
   black pepper
2½ cups chicken stock

7 slices stale white bread
¼ medium cucumber, diced
4 whole basil leaves

Make a small cross in the bottom of each tomato, then place in a bowl and cover with boiling water. Let stand for 2 minutes, or until the skins have started to peel away, then drain, remove the skins and seeds, and chop into large pieces.

Heat 3 tablespoons of the olive oil in a saucepan and gently cook the onion until softened. Add the skinned tomatoes, chopped basil, garlic, and chili powder, and season to taste with salt and pepper. Pour in the stock, cover the saucepan, bring to a boil, and simmer gently for 15–20 minutes.

Remove the crusts from the bread and break into small pieces. Remove the tomato mixture from the heat and stir in the bread. Cover and let stand for 10 minutes, or until the bread has blended with the tomatoes. Season to taste. Serve warm or cold with a swirl of olive oil on the top, garnished with a spoonful of chopped cucumber and basil leaves.

Chinese Omelette

SERVES 1

½ cup bean sprouts
1 medium carrot, peeled and
  cut into matchsticks
½ inch piece root ginger,
  peeled and grated
1 tsp soy sauce

2 large eggs
salt and freshly ground black
  pepper
1 tbsp dark sesame oil

To serve:
tossed green salad
soy sauce

Lightly rinse the bean sprouts, then place in the top of a bamboo steamer with the carrots. Add the grated ginger and soy sauce. Set the steamer over a pan or wok half-filled with gently simmering water and steam for 10 minutes, or until the vegetables are tender but still crisp. Reserve and keep warm.

Whisk the eggs in a bowl until frothy and season to taste with salt and pepper. Heat an 8-inch omelette pan or skillet and add the sesame oil; when hot, pour in the beaten eggs. Whisk the eggs around with a fork, then let them cook and start to set. When the top surface starts to bubble, tilt the edges to allow the uncooked egg to run underneath.

Spoon the bean sprout and carrot mixture over the top of the omelette and let it cook a little longer. When it has set, slide the omelette onto a warmed serving dish and carefully roll up. Serve immediately with a tossed green salad and extra soy sauce.

Try this: FOR MAIN MEAL: 180 FOR DESSERT: 354

Rice & Tomato Soup

SERVES 4

¾ cup basmati rice
14-oz can chopped tomatoes
2 garlic cloves, peeled
   and crushed
grated rind of ½ lime
2 tbsp extra virgin olive oil

1 tsp sugar
salt and freshly
   ground pepper
1¼ cups vegetable stock
   or water

For the croutons:
2 tbsp prepared pesto sauce
2 tbsp olive oil
6 thin slices ciabatta bread,
   cut into ½-inch cubes

Preheat the oven to 425°F. Rinse and drain the basmati rice. Place the canned tomatoes with their juice in a large heavy-based saucepan with the garlic, lime rind, oil, and sugar. Season to taste with salt and pepper. Bring to a boil, reduce the heat, cover, and simmer for 10 minutes.

Add the boiling vegetable stock or water and the rice, then cook, uncovered, for a further 15–20 minutes, or until the rice is tender. If the soup is too thick, add a little more water. Reserve and keep warm, if the croutons are not ready.

Meanwhile, to make the croutons, mix the pesto and olive oil in a large bowl. Add the bread cubes and toss until they are coated completely with the mixture. Spread on a baking sheet and bake in the preheated oven for 10–15 minutes, until golden and crisp, turning them over halfway through cooking. Serve the soup immediately sprinkled with the warm croutons.

Try this: FOR MAIN MEAL: 124   FOR DESSERT: 372

Chicken & Lamb Satay

MAKES 16

8 oz skinless, boneless
    chicken
8 oz lean lamb

For the marinade:
1 small onion, peeled
    and finely chopped
2 garlic cloves, peeled
    and crushed
1-inch piece fresh ginger,
    peeled and grated

4 tbsp soy sauce
1 tsp coriander
2 tsp dark brown sugar
2 tbsp lime juice
1 tbsp vegetable oil

For the peanut sauce:
1¼ cups coconut milk
4 tbsp crunchy peanut butter
1 tbsp Thai fish sauce
1 tsp lime juice

1 tbsp chili powder
1 tbsp brown sugar
salt and freshly ground
    black pepper

To garnish:
sprigs of fresh cilantro
lime wedges

Preheat the broiler just before cooking. Soak the bamboo skewers for 30 minutes before required. Cut the chicken and lamb into thin strips about 3 inches long and place in 2 shallow dishes. Blend all the marinade ingredients together, then pour half over the chicken and half over the lamb. Stir until lightly coated, then cover with plastic wrap and let marinate in the refrigerator for at least 2 hours, turning occasionally.

Remove the chicken and lamb from the marinade and thread onto the skewers. Reserve the marinade. Cook under the preheated broiler for 8–10 minutes, or until cooked, turning and brushing with the marinade.

Meanwhile, make the peanut sauce. Blend the coconut milk with the peanut butter, fish sauce, lime juice, chili powder, and sugar. Pour into a saucepan and cook gently for 5 minutes, stirring occasionally, then season to taste with salt and pepper. Garnish with cilantro sprigs and lime wedges and serve the satays with the prepared sauce.

Potato & Fennel Soup

SERVES 4

2 tbsp butter
2 large onions, peeled
  and thinly sliced
2–3 garlic cloves, peeled
  and crushed
1 tsp salt
2 medium potatoes (about

1 lb), peeled and diced
1 fennel bulb, trimmed
  and finely chopped
½ tsp caraway seeds
4¼ cups vegetable stock
freshly ground
  black pepper

2 tbsp freshly
  chopped parsley
4 tbsp crème fraîche
  or sour cream
roughly torn pieces of
  French bread, to serve

Melt the butter in a large, heavy-based saucepan. Add the onions, with the garlic and half the salt, and cook over a medium heat, stirring occasionally, for 7–10 minutes, or until the onions are soft and beginning to turn brown.

Add the potatoes, fennel bulb, caraway seeds, and the remaining salt. Cook for about 5 minutes, then pour in the vegetable stock. Bring to a boil, partially cover, and simmer for 15–20 minutes, or until the potatoes are tender. Stir in the chopped parsley and adjust the seasoning to taste.

For a smooth-textured soup, let cool slightly then pour into a food processor or blender and blend until smooth. Reheat the soup gently, then ladle into individual soup bowls. For a chunky soup, omit this blending stage and ladle straight from the saucepan into soup bowls.

Swirl a spoonful of crème fraîche into each bowl and serve immediately with roughly torn pieces of French bread.

Try this: FOR MAIN MEAL: 150   FOR DESSERT: 352

Main Meals

Mediterranean Fish Stew

SERVES 4-6

4 tbsp olive oil
1 onion, peeled and
    finely sliced
5 garlic cloves, peeled
    and finely sliced
1 fennel bulb, trimmed
    and finely chopped
3 celery sticks, trimmed
    and finely chopped

14-oz can chopped tomatoes
    with Italian herbs
1 tbsp freshly
    chopped oregano
1 bay leaf
zest and juice of 1 orange
1 tsp saffron strands
3 cups fish stock
3 tbsp dry vermouth

salt and freshly ground
    black pepper
8 oz thick haddock fillets
8 oz sea bass or bream fillets
8 oz raw, large shrimp,
    peeled
crusty bread, to serve

Heat the olive oil in a large saucepan. Add the onion, garlic, fennel, and celery, and cook over a low heat for 15 minutes, stirring frequently until the vegetables are soft and just beginning to turn brown.

Add the canned tomatoes with their juices, oregano, bay leaf, orange zest and juice, and the saffron strands. Bring to a boil, then reduce the heat and simmer for 5 minutes. Add the fish stock and vermouth, and season to taste with salt and pepper. Bring to a boil. Reduce the heat and simmer for 20 minutes.

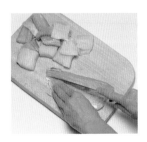

Wipe or rinse the haddock and bass fillets and remove as many of the bones as possible. Place on a cutting board and cut into 2-inch cubes. Add to the saucepan and cook for 3 minutes. Add the shrimp and cook for a further 5 minutes. Adjust the seasoning to taste and serve with crusty bread.

Try this: FOR AN APPETIZER: 18   FOR DESSERT: 352

Pea & Shrimp Risotto

SERVES 6

1 lb whole raw shrimp
½ cup (1 stick) butter
1 red onion, peeled
   and chopped
4 garlic cloves, peeled

and finely chopped
1 cup Arborio rice
⅔ cup dry white wine
4½ cups vegetable
   or fish stock

2 cups frozen peas
4 tbsp freshly
   chopped mint
salt and freshly ground
   black pepper

Peel the shrimp and reserve the heads and shells. Remove the black vein from the back of each shrimp, then wash and dry on a paper towel. Melt half the butter in a large skillet, add the shrimp heads and shells, and fry, stirring occasionally for 3–4 minutes, or until golden. Strain the butter, discard the heads and shells, and return the butter to the pan.

Add a further 2 tablespoons of butter to the skillet and fry the onion and garlic for 5 minutes until softened, but not colored. Add the rice and stir the grains in the butter for 1 minute, until they are coated thoroughly. Add the white wine and boil rapidly until the wine reduces by half.

Bring the stock to a gentle simmer, and add to the rice, one ladleful at a time. Stir constantly, adding the stock as it is absorbed, until the rice is creamy but still has a bite in the center.

Melt the remaining butter and stir-fry the shrimp for 3–4 minutes. Stir into the rice, along with all the pan juices and the peas. Add the chopped mint and season to taste with salt and pepper. Cover the pan and let stand for 5 minutes before serving.

Try this: FOR AN APPETIZER: 40   FOR DESSERT: 364

Cod with Fennel & Cardamom

SERVES 4

1 garlic clove, peeled
  and crushed
finely grated rind of 1 lemon
1 tsp lemon juice

1 tbsp olive oil
1 fennel bulb
1 tbsp cardamom pods
salt and freshly ground

black pepper
4 x 6-oz thick cod fillets

Preheat the oven to 375°F. Place the garlic in a small bowl with the lemon rind, lemon juice, and olive oil and stir well.

Cover and let stand for at least 30 minutes. Stir well before using.

Trim the fennel bulb, thinly slice it, and place in a bowl.

Place the cardamom pods in a pestle and mortar and lightly pound to crack the pods. Alternatively place in a plastic bag and pound gently with a rolling pin. Add the crushed cardamom to the fennel slices.

Season the fish with salt and pepper and place onto 4 separate 8 x 8-inch parchment paper squares.

Spoon the fennel mixture over the fish and drizzle with the infused oil.

Place the parcels on a baking sheet and bake in the preheated oven for 8–10 minutes, or until cooked. Serve immediately in the paper parcels.

Try this: FOR AN APPETIZER: 20 FOR DESSERT: 354

Gingered Cod Steaks

SERVES 4

1-inch piece fresh ginger,
    peeled
4 green onions
2 tsp freshly
    chopped parsley

1 tbsp brown sugar
4 x 6 oz thick cod steaks
salt and freshly ground
    black pepper
2 tbsp butter

freshly cooked vegetables,
    to serve

Preheat the broiler and line the broiler rack with a layer of foil. Coarsely grate the piece of ginger. Trim the green onions and cut into thin strips.

Mix the green onions, ginger, chopped parsley, and sugar. Add 1 tablespoon of water.

Wipe the fish steaks. Season to taste with salt and pepper. Place on to 4 separate 8 x 8-inch foil squares.

Carefully spoon the green onions and ginger mixture over the fish.

Cut the butter into small cubes and place over the fish.

Loosely fold the foil over the steaks to enclose the fish and to make a parcel.

Place under the preheated broiler and cook for 10–12 minutes, or until cooked and the flesh has turned opaque.

Place the fish parcels on individual serving plates. Serve immediately with the freshly cooked vegetables.

Try this: FOR AN APPETIZER: 24   FOR DESSERT: 356

Sardines with Red Currants

SERVES 4

2 tbsp red currant jelly
finely grated rind of 1 lime
2 tbsp medium-dry sherry
1 lb fresh sardines, cleaned
   and heads removed

sea salt and freshly ground
   black pepper
lime wedges,
   to garnish

To serve:
fresh red currants
fresh green salad

Preheat the broiler and line the broiler rack with foil 2–3 minutes before cooking.

Warm the red currant jelly in a bowl standing over a pan of gently simmering water and stir until smooth. Add the lime rind and sherry to the bowl and stir well until blended.

Lightly rinse the sardines and pat dry with a paper towel.

Place on a cutting board, and with a sharp knife, make several diagonal cuts across the flesh of each fish. Season the sardines inside the cavities with salt and pepper.

Gently brush the warm marinade over the skin and inside the cavities of the sardines.

Place on the broiler rack and cook under the preheated broiler for 8–10 minutes, or until the fish are cooked.

Carefully turn the sardines over at least once during broiling. Baste occasionally with the remaining red currant and lime marinade. Garnish with the red currants. Serve immediately with the salad and lime wedges.

Try this: FOR AN APPETIZER: 56 FOR DESSERT: 372

Hot Salsa–filled Sole

SERVES 4

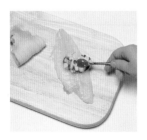

8 x 6 oz lemon sole fillets,
   skinned
⅔ cup orange juice
2 tbsp lemon juice

For the salsa:
1 small mango

8 cherry tomatoes,
   quartered
1 small red onion, peeled
   and finely chopped
pinch of sugar
1 red chile pepper
2 tbsp rice vinegar

zest and juice of 1 lime
1 tbsp olive oil
sea salt and freshly ground
   black pepper
2 tbsp freshly chopped mint
lime wedges, to garnish
salad leaves, to serve

First make the salsa. Peel the mango and cut the flesh away from the stone. Chop finely and place in a small bowl. Add the cherry tomatoes, onion, and sugar to the mango.

Cut the top of the chile pepper. Slit down the side and discard the seeds and the membrane (the skin to which the seeds are attached). Finely chop the chile pepper and add to the mango mixture with the vinegar, lime zest and juice, and oil. Season to taste with salt and pepper. Mix thoroughly and let stand for 30 minutes to allow the flavors to develop.

Lay the fish fillets on a board, skinned-side up, and pile the salsa on the tail end of the fillets. Fold the fillets in half, season, and place in a large shallow skillet. Pour over the orange and lemon juice.

Bring to a gentle boil, then reduce the heat to a simmer. Cover and cook on a low heat for 7–10 minutes, adding a little water if the liquid is evaporating. Remove the cover, add the mint, and cook uncovered for a further 3 minutes. Garnish with lime wedges and serve immediately with the salad.

Try this: FOR AN APPETIZER: 30   FOR DESSERT: 380

Zesty Whole–baked Fish

SERVES 8

4 lb whole salmon, cleaned
sea salt and freshly ground
   black pepper
¼ cup low-fat margarine
1 garlic clove, peeled
   and finely sliced
zest and juice of 1 lemon

zest of 1 orange
1 tsp freshly grated nutmeg
3 tbsp Dijon mustard
2 tbsp fresh
   white bread crumbs
2 bunches fresh dill
1 bunch fresh tarragon

1 lime sliced
⅔ cup semi-fat crème fraîche
   or sour cream
2 cups whole-fat
   plain yogurt
dill sprigs, to garnish

Preheat the oven to 425°F. Lightly rinse the fish and pat dry with a paper towel. Season the cavity with a little salt and pepper. Make several diagonal cuts across the flesh of the fish and season.

Mix together the margarine, garlic, lemon and orange zest and juice, nutmeg, mustard, and fresh bread crumbs. Mix well together. Spoon the bread-crumb mixture into the slits with a small sprig of dill. Place the remaining herbs inside the fish cavity. Weigh the fish and calculate the cooking time. Allow 10 minutes per pound.

Lay the fish on a double thickness foil. If you want, smear the fish with a little low-fat margarine. Top with the lime slices and fold the foil into a parcel. Chill in the refrigerator for 15 minutes.

Place in a roasting pan and cook in the preheated oven for the calculated cooking time. About 15 minutes before the end of cooking, open the foil and return until the skin begins to crisp. Remove the fish from the oven and let stand for 10 minutes.

Pour the juices from the roasting pan into a saucepan. Bring to a boil and stir in the crème fraîche and yogurt. Simmer for 3 minutes or until hot. Garnish with dill sprigs and serve immediately.

 Try this: FOR AN APPETIZER: 26   FOR DESSERT: 358

Fish Crumble

SERVES 6

1 lb whiting or
  halibut fillets
1¼ cups milk
salt and freshly ground
  black pepper
1 tbsp sunflower oil
6 tbsp butter or margarine
1 medium onion, peeled
  and finely chopped

2 leeks, trimmed and sliced
1 medium carrot, peeled
  and diced
2 medium potatoes, peeled
  and cut into small pieces
1½ cups all-purpose flour
1¼ cups fish or vegetable
  stock
2 tbsp heavy cream

1 tsp freshly chopped dill
snap beans, to serve

For the crumble topping:
6 tbsp butter or margarine
1½ cups all-purpose flour
3 cups Parmesan cheese,
  grated
¾ tsp cayenne pepper

Preheat the oven to 400°F, 15 minutes before cooking. Oil a shallow casserole dish. Place the fish in a saucepan with the milk, salt, and pepper. Bring to a boil, cover, and simmer for 8–10 minutes, until the fish is cooked. Remove with a slotted spoon, reserving the cooking liquid. Flake the fish into the prepared dish.

Heat the oil and 1 tablespoon of the butter or margarine in a small skillet and gently fry the onion, leeks, carrot, and potatoes for 1–2 minutes. Cover tightly and cook over a gentle heat for a further 10 minutes until softened. Spoon the vegetables over the fish.

Melt the remaining butter or margarine in a saucepan, add the flour, and cook for 1 minute, stirring. Whisk in the reserved cooking liquid and the stock. Cook until thickened, then stir in the cream. Remove from the heat and stir in the dill. Pour over the fish.

To make the crumble, rub the butter or margarine into the flour until it resembles breadcrumbs, then stir in the cheese and cayenne pepper. Sprinkle over the dish, and bake in the preheated oven for 20 minutes until piping hot. Serve with snap beans.

Try this: FOR AN APPETIZER: 64   FOR DESSERT: 370

Roasted Cod with Saffron Aïoli

SERVES 4

For the saffron aïoli:
2 garlic cloves, peeled
¼ tsp saffron strands
sea salt, to taste
1 medium egg yolk
1 cup extra-virgin
    olive oil
2 tbsp lemon juice

For the marinade:
2 tbsp olive oil
4 garlic cloves, peeled and
    finely chopped
1 red onion, peeled and
    finely chopped
1 tbsp freshly chopped
    rosemary

2 tbsp freshly
    chopped thyme
4–6 sprigs of fresh rosemary
1 lemon, sliced
6 oz thick cod fillets with skin
freshly cooked vegtables,
    to serve

Preheat the oven to 350°F, 10 minutes before cooking. Crush the garlic, saffron, and a pinch of salt in a pestle and mortar to form a paste. Place in a blender with the egg yolk and blend for 30 seconds. With the motor running, slowly add the olive oil in a thin, steady stream until the mayonnaise is smooth and thick. Spoon into a small bowl and stir in the lemon juice. Cover and refrigerate until required.

Combine the olive oil, garlic, red onion, rosemary, and thyme for the marinade and let stand for about 10 minutes.

Place the sprigs of rosemary and slices of lemon in the bottom of a lightly oiled roasting pan. Add the cod, skinned-side up. Pour over the prepared marinade and let marinate in the refrigerator for 15–20 minutes. Bake in the preheated oven for 15–20 minutes, or until the cod is cooked and the flesh flakes easily with a fork. Leave the cod to rest for 1 minute before serving with the saffron aïoli and vegetables.

Try this: FOR AN APPETIZER: 60 FOR DESSERT: 354

Salmon & Mushroom Linguine

SERVES 4

1 lb salmon
    fillets, skinned
salt and freshly ground
    black pepper
6 tbsp butter
6 tbsp flour

1¼ cups chicken stock
⅔ cup heavy cream
3¼ cups button mushrooms,
    cleaned and sliced
12 oz linguine
½ cup Cheddar

cheese, grated
½ cup fresh white bread
    crumbs
2 tbsp freshly chopped
    parsley, to garnish

Preheat the oven to 375˚F, 10 minutes before cooking. Place the salmon in a shallow pan and cover with water. Season well with salt and pepper and bring to a boil, then lower the heat and simmer for 6–8 minutes, or until cooked. Drain and keep warm.

Melt 4 tablespoons of the butter in a heavy-based pan, stir in the flour, cook for 1 minute, then whisk in the chicken stock. Simmer gently until thickened. Stir in the cream and season to taste. Keep the sauce warm.

Melt the remaining butter in a pan, add the sliced mushrooms, and cook for 2–3 minutes. Stir the mushrooms into the white sauce.

Bring a large pan of lightly salted water to a rapid boil. Add the linguine and cook according to the package instructions, or until cooked but still firm.

Drain the pasta thoroughly and return to the pan. Stir in half the sauce, then spoon into a lightly oiled a shallow ovenproof dish. Flake the salmon, add to the remaining sauce, then pour over the pasta. Sprinkle with the cheese and bread crumbs, then bake in the preheated oven for 15–20 minutes, or until golden. Garnish with the parsley and serve immediately.

Try this: FOR AN APPETIZER: 20 FOR DESSERT: 362

Tuna Cannelloni

SERVES 4

1 tbsp olive oil
6 green onions, trimmed
   and finely sliced
1 sweet red bell pepper,
   deseeded and finely
   chopped
7 oz can tuna in brine

1 cup ricotta cheese
zest and juice of 1 lemon
1 tbsp freshly snipped chives
salt and freshly ground
   black pepper
8 dried cannelloni tubes
1 medium egg, beaten

½ cup cottage cheese
⅔ cup plain yogurt
pinch of freshly grated
   nutmeg
½ cup mozzarella
   cheese, grated
tossed green salad, to serve

Preheat the oven to 375˚F, 10 minutes before cooking. Heat the olive oil in a skillet and cook the green onions and pepper until soft. Remove from the skillet with a slotted draining spoon and place in large bowl.

Drain the tuna, then stir into the green onions and pepper. Beat the ricotta cheese with the lemon zest and juice and the snipped chives until soft and blended. Season to taste with salt and pepper, add to the tuna, and mix together. If the mixture is still a little stiff, add a little extra lemon juice.

With a teaspoon, carefully spoon the mixture into the cannelloni tubes, then lay the filled tubes in a lightly oiled shallow ovenproof dish. Beat the egg, cottage cheese, plain yogurt, and nutmeg together and pour over the cannelloni. Sprinkle with the grated mozzarella cheese and bake in the preheated oven for 15–20 minutes, or until the topping is golden brown and bubbling. Serve immediately with a tossed green salad.

Try this: FOR AN APPETIZER: 32   FOR DESSERT: 350

Grilled Red Mullet with Orange & Anchovy Sauce

SERVES 4

2 oranges
4 x 6 oz red mullet, cleaned
   and descaled
salt and freshly ground
   black pepper
4 sprigs of fresh rosemary

1 lemon, sliced
2 tbsp olive oil
2 garlic cloves, peeled
   and crushed
6 anchovy fillets in
   oil, drained and

roughly chopped
2 tsp freshly chopped
   rosemary
1 tsp lemon juice

Preheat the broiler and line the broiler rack with foil just before cooking. Peel the oranges with a sharp knife, over a bowl to catch the juice. Cut into thin slices and reserve. If necessary, make up the juice to ⅔ cup with extra juice.

Place the fish on a cutting board and make two diagonal slashes across the thickest part of both sides of each fish. Season well, both inside and out, with salt and pepper. Tuck a rosemary sprig and a few lemon slices inside the cavity of each fish. Brush the fish with a little of the olive oil and then cook under the preheated broiler for 4–5 minutes on each side. The flesh should just fall away from the bone.

Heat the remaining oil in a saucepan and gently fry the garlic and anchovies for 3–4 minutes. Do not allow to brown. Add the chopped rosemary and plenty of black pepper. The anchovies will be salty enough, so do not add any salt. Stir in the orange slices with their juice and the lemon juice. Simmer gently until heated through. Spoon the sauce over the red mullet and serve immediately.

Try this: FOR AN APPETIZER: 28   FOR DESSERT: 352

Chili Monkfish Stir-Fry

SERVES 4

12 oz pasta twists
1¼ lb monkfish, trimmed
    and cut into chunks
2 tbsp peanut oil
1 green chile pepper,
    deseeded and cut
    into matchsticks

2 tbsp sesame seeds
pinch of cayenne pepper
sliced green chile peppers,
    to garnish

For the marinade:
1 garlic clove, peeled

    and chopped
2 tbsp dark soy sauce
grated zest and juice
    of 1 lime
1 tbsp sweet chili sauce
4 tbsp olive oil

Bring a large saucepan of lightly salted water to a rapid boil and add the pasta. Stir, bring back to a boil, and cook at for 8 minutes, or until cooked but still firm. Drain thoroughly and reserve.

For the marinade, mix together the chopped garlic, dark soy sauce, lime zest and juice, sweet chili sauce, and olive oil in a shallow dish, then add the monkfish chunks. Stir until all the monkfish is lightly coated in the marinade, then cover and refrigerate for at least 30 minutes, spooning the marinade over the fish occasionally.

Heat a wok, then add the oil and heat until almost smoking. Remove the monkfish from the marinade, scraping off as much marinade as possible, add to the wok and stir-fry for 3 minutes. Add the green chile pepper and sesame seeds, and stir-fry the mixture for a further minute.

Stir in the pasta and marinade, and stir-fry for 1–2 minutes, or until piping hot. Sprinkle with cayenne pepper and garnish with sliced green chile peppers. Serve immediately.

Try this: FOR AN APPETIZER: 24 FOR DESSERT: 368

Grilled Snapper with Roasted Pepper

SERVES 4

1 medium red bell pepper
1 medium green bell pepper
4–8 snapper fillets (about
   1 lb in total)
sea salt and freshly

ground black pepper
1 tbsp olive oil
5 tbsp heavy cream
½ cup white wine
1 tbsp freshly chopped dill

sprigs of fresh dill,
   to garnish
freshly cooked tagliatelle,
   to serve

Preheat the broiler to a high heat and line the broiler rack with foil. Cut the tops off the peppers and divide into quarters. Remove the seeds and the membrane, then place on the foil-lined broiler rack and cook for 8–10 minutes, turning frequently, until the skins have become charred and blackened. Remove from the broiler rack, place in a plastic bag, and let cool. When the peppers are cool, strip off the skin, slice thinly, and reserve.

Cover the broiler rack with another piece of foil, then place the snapper fillets, skin-side up, on the broiler rack. Season to taste with salt and pepper and brush with a little of the olive oil. Cook for 10–12 minutes, turning over once and brushing again with a little olive oil.

Pour the cream and wine into a small saucepan, bring to a boil and simmer for about 5 minutes, until the sauce has thickened slightly. Add the dill, season to taste, and stir in the sliced peppers. Arrange the cooked snapper fillets on warm serving plates and pour over the cream and pepper sauce. Garnish with sprigs of dill and serve immediately with freshly cooked tagliatelle.

Try this: FOR AN APPETIZER: 18 FOR DESSERT: 356

Chinese Five Spice Marinated Salmon

SERVES 4

1½ lb skinless salmon fillet,
    cut into 1-inch strips
2 medium egg whites
1 tbsp cornstarch
vegetable oil for frying
4 green onions, cut
    diagonally into
    2-inch pieces

½ cup fish stock
lime or lemon wedges,
    to garnish

For the marinade:
3 tbsp soy sauce
3 tbsp Chinese rice wine
    or dry sherry

2 tsp sesame oil
1 tbsp brown sugar
1 tbsp lime or lemon juice
1 tsp Chinese five
    spice powder
2–3 dashes hot
    pepper sauce

Combine the marinade ingredients in a shallow nonmetallic baking dish until well blended. Add the salmon strips and stir gently to coat. Let marinate in the refrigerator for 20–30 minutes.

Using a slotted spoon, remove the salmon pieces, drain on a paper towel, and pat dry. Reserve the marinade.

Beat the egg whites with the cornstarch to make a batter. Add the salmon strips and stir into the batter until coated completely.

Pour enough oil into a large wok to come 2 inches up the side and place over a high heat. Working in 2 or 3 batches, add the salmon strips and cook for 1–2 minutes, or until golden. Remove from the wok with a slotted spoon and drain on a paper towel. Reserve.

Discard the hot oil and wipe the wok clean. Add the marinade, green onions, and stock to the wok. Bring to a boil and simmer for 1 minute. Add the salmon strips and stir-fry gently until coated in the sauce. Spoon into a warmed shallow serving dish, garnish with the lime or lemon wedges, and serve immediately.

Try this: FOR AN APPETIZER: 36   FOR DESSERT: 374

Saucy Cod & Pasta Bake

SERVES 4

1 lb cod fillets, skinned
2 tbsp sunflower oil
1 onion, peeled and chopped
4 slices smoked, streaky
   bacon, rind removed
   and chopped
2 cups baby button
   mushrooms, cleaned
2 celery sticks, trimmed
   and thinly sliced

2 small zucchini, halved
   lengthwise and sliced
14-oz can chopped tomatoes
½ cup fish stock
   or dry white wine
1 tbsp freshly
   chopped tarragon
salt and freshly ground
   black pepper

For the pasta topping:
8–10 oz pasta shells
2 tbsp butter
4 tbsp all-purpose flour
2 cups milk

Preheat the oven to 400°F, 15 minutes before cooking. Cut the cod into bite-sized pieces and reserve. Heat the sunflower oil in a large saucepan, add the onion and bacon, and cook for 7–8 minutes. Add the mushrooms and celery and cook for 5 minutes, or until fairly soft.

Add the zucchini and tomatoes to the bacon mixture and pour in the fish stock or wine. Bring to a boil, then simmer uncovered for 5 minutes, or until the sauce has thickened slightly. Remove from the heat and stir in the cod pieces and the tarragon. Season to taste with salt and pepper, then spoon into a large oiled baking dish.

Meanwhile, bring a large pan of lightly salted water to a rapid boil. Add the pasta shells and cook, according to the package instructions, or until cooked but still firm.

For the topping, place the butter and flour in a saucepan and pour in the milk. Bring to a boil slowly, whisking until thickened and smooth. Drain the pasta thoroughly, and stir into the sauce. Spoon carefully over the fish and vegetables. Place in the preheated oven and bake for 20–25 minutes, or until the top is lightly browned and bubbling.

Try this: FOR AN APPETIZER: 46   FOR DESSERT: 362

Tagliatelle with Tuna & Anchovy Tapenade

SERVES 4

14 oz tagliatelle
4½-oz can tuna fish in
  oil, drained
1¾-oz can anchovy fillets,
  drained

35 pitted, large black olives
2 tbsp capers in
  brine, drained
2 tsp lemon juice
½ cup olive oil

2 tbsp freshly
  chopped parsley
freshly ground black pepper
sprigs of flat-leaf parsley,
  to garnish

Bring a large pan of lightly salted water to a rapid boil. Add the tagliatelle and cook according to the package instructions, or until cooked but still firm.

Meanwhile, place the tuna fish, anchovy fillets, olives, and capers in a food processor with the lemon juice and 2 tablespoons of the olive oil and blend for a few seconds until roughly chopped.

With the motor running, pour in the remaining olive oil in a steady stream; the resulting mixture should be slightly chunky rather than smooth.

Spoon the sauce into a bowl, stir in the chopped parsley, and season to taste with black pepper. Check the taste of the sauce and add a little more lemon juice, if required.

Drain the pasta thoroughly. Pour the sauce into the pan and cook over a low heat for 1–2 minutes to warm through.

Return the drained pasta to the pan and mix together with the sauce. Tip into a warmed serving bowl or spoon onto warm individual plates. Garnish with sprigs of flat-leaf parsley and serve immediately.

Try this: FOR AN APPETIZER: 32 FOR DESSERT: 352

Spicy Shrimp Noodles with Sesame Dressing

SERVES 4

2½ cups vegetable stock
12 oz Chinese egg noodles
1 tbsp sunflower oil
1 garlic clove, peeled
   and finely chopped
1 red chile pepper,

deseeded and
   finely chopped
3 tbsp sesame seeds
3 tbsp dark soy sauce
2 tbsp sesame oil
6 oz shelled, cooked shrimp

3 tbsp freshly chopped
   cilantro
freshly ground black pepper
fresh cilantro sprigs,
   to garnish

Pour the vegetable stock into a large saucepan and bring to a boil. Add the egg noodles, stir once, then cook according to the package instructions, usually about 3 minutes.

Meanwhile, heat the sunflower oil in a small skillet. Add the chopped garlic and chile pepper and cook gently for a few seconds. Add the sesame seeds and cook, stirring continuously, for 1 minute, or until golden.

Add the soy sauce, sesame oil, and shrimp to the skillet. Continue cooking for a few seconds, until the mixture is just starting to bubble, then remove immediately from the heat.

Drain the noodles thoroughly and return to the pan. Add the shrimp, along with the dressing mixture, and the chopped cilantro, and season to taste with black pepper. Toss gently to coat the noodles with the hot dressing.

Tip into a warmed serving bowl or spoon on to individual plates and serve immediately, garnished with sprigs of fresh cilantro.

Try this: FOR AN APPETIZER: 24 FOR DESSERT: 378

Chinese–style Fried Rice

SERVES 4-6

2–3 tbsp peanut oil
  or vegetable oil
2 small onions, peeled
  and cut into wedges
2 garlic cloves, peeled
  and thinly sliced
10-inch piece of fresh ginger,
  peeled and cut into slivers
8 oz cooked chicken,
  thinly sliced
4 oz cooked ham,
  thinly sliced

2½ cups cooked, cold,
  long-grain white rice
5-oz can water chestnuts,
  sliced
8 oz cooked, peeled shrimp
  (optional)
3 large eggs
3 tsp sesame oil
salt and freshly ground
  black pepper
6 green onions, trimmed
  and sliced into ½-inch

pieces
2 tbsp dark soy sauce
1 tbsp sweet chili sauce
2 tbsp freshly
  chopped cilantro

To garnish:
2 tbsp chopped roasted
  peanuts
sprig of fresh cilantro

Heat a wok or large, deep skillet until hot, add the oil, and heat for 30 seconds. Add the onions and stir-fry for 2 minutes. Stir in the garlic and ginger and cook for 1 minute. Add the cooked sliced chicken and ham and stir-fry for a further 2–3 minutes.

Add the rice, the water chestnuts, and shrimp, if using, with 2 tablespoons of water, and stir-fry for 2 minutes until the rice is heated through.

Beat the eggs with 1 teaspoon of the sesame oil and season to taste with salt and pepper. Make a well in the center of the rice, then pour in the egg mixture and stir immediately, gradually drawing the rice mixture into the egg, until the egg is cooked.

Add the green onions, soy and chili sauces, cilantro, and a little water, if necessary. Adjust the seasoning and drizzle with the remaining sesame oil. Sprinkle with the nuts and serve.

Try this: FOR AN APPETIZER: 48   FOR DESSERT: 354

Oven–roasted Vegetables with Sausages

SERVES 4

2 medium eggplants,
    trimmed
3 medium zucchini, trimmed
4 tbsp olive oil
6 garlic cloves
8 Tuscany-style sausages

4 plum tomatoes
2 x 10½-oz can
    cannellini beans
salt and freshly ground
    black pepper
1 bunch of fresh basil,

    torn into coarse pieces
1 cup Parmesan
    cheese, grated

Preheat the oven to 400˚F, 15 minutes before cooking. Cut the eggplants and zucchini into bite-sized chunks. Place the olive oil in a large roasting pan and heat in the preheated oven for 3 minutes, or until hot. Add the eggplants, zucchini, and garlic cloves, then stir until coated in the hot oil and cook in the oven for 10 minutes.

Remove the roasting pan from the oven and stir. Lightly prick the sausages, add to the roasting pan, and return to the oven. Continue to roast for a further 20 minutes, turning once during cooking, until the vegetables are tender and the sausages are golden brown.

Meanwhile, roughly chop the plum tomatoes and drain the cannellini beans. Remove the sausages from the oven and stir in the tomatoes and cannellini beans. Season to taste with salt and pepper, then return to the oven for 5 minutes, or until heated thoroughly.

Scatter over the basil leaves and sprinkle with plenty of Parmesan cheese and extra freshly ground black pepper. Serve immediately.

Try this: FOR AN APPETIZER: 40 FOR DESSERT: 356

Pork Sausages with Onion Gravy & Best-ever Mash

SERVES 4

4 tbsp butter
1 tbsp olive oil
2 large onions, peeled
  and thinly sliced
pinch of sugar
1 tbsp freshly chopped thyme
1 tbsp all-purpose flour
½ cup Madeira

1 cup vegetable stock
8–12 good-quality pork
  sausages, depending
  on size

For the mash:
6 medium floury
  potatoes (about 2 lb),

  peeled
6 tbsp butter
4 tbsp crème fraîche
  or sour cream
salt and freshly ground
  black pepper

Melt the butter with the oil and add the onions. Cover and cook gently for about 20 minutes until the onions have collapsed. Add the sugar and stir well. Uncover and continue to cook, stirring often, until the onions are soft and golden. Add the thyme, stir well, then add the flour, stirring. Gradually add the Madeira and the stock. Bring to a boil and simmer gently for 10 minutes.

Meanwhile, put the sausages in a large skillet and cook over a medium heat for about 15–20 minutes, turning often, until golden brown and slightly sticky all over.

For the mash, boil the potatoes in plenty of lightly salted water for 15–18 minutes, until tender. Drain well and return to the saucepan. Put the saucepan over a low heat to allow the potatoes to dry thoroughly. Remove from the heat and add the butter, crème fraîche, and salt and pepper. Mash thoroughly. Serve the potato mash topped with the sausages and onion gravy.

Try this: FOR AN APPETIZER: 38   FOR DESSERT: 366

Sausage & Red Currant Pasta Bake

SERVES 4

1 lb good-quality,
   thick pork sausages
2 tsp sunflower oil
2 tbsp butter
1 onion, peeled and sliced
2 tbsp all-purpose flour
2 cups chicken stock

⅔ cup port or good-quality
   red wine
1 tbsp freshly chopped
   thyme leaves, plus
   sprigs to garnish
1 bay leaf
4 tbsp red currant jelly

salt and freshly ground
   black pepper
12 oz fresh penne
¾ cup Gruyère cheese,
   grated

Preheat the oven to 425°F, 15 minutes before cooking. Prick the sausages, place in a shallow ovenproof dish and toss in the sunflower oil. Cook in the oven for 25–30 minutes, or until golden brown.

Meanwhile, melt the butter in a skillet, add the sliced onion, and fry for 5 minutes, or until golden brown. Stir in the flour and cook for 2 minutes. Remove the pan from the heat and gradually stir in the chicken stock with the port or red wine.

Return the pan to the heat and bring to a boil, stirring continuously until the sauce starts to thicken. Add the thyme, bay leaf, and red currant jelly, and season well with salt and pepper. Simmer the sauce for 5 minutes. Bring a large pan of salted water to a rapid boil, add the pasta, and cook for about 4 minutes, or until cooked but still firm. Drain thoroughly and reserve.

Lower the oven temperature to 400°F. Remove the sausages from the oven, drain off any excess fat, and return the sausages to the dish. Add the pasta. Pour over the sauce, removing the bay leaf, and toss together. Sprinkle with the Gruyère cheese and return to the oven for 15–20 minutes, or until bubbling and golden brown. Serve immediately, garnished with thyme sprigs.

Try this: FOR AN APPETIZER: 56   FOR DESSERT: 372

Spanish–style Pork Stew with Saffron Rice

SERVES 4

2 tbsp olive oil
2 lb boneless pork shoulder, diced
1 large onion, peeled and sliced
2 garlic cloves, peeled and finely chopped
1 tbsp all-purpose flour
7–8 plum tomatoes (about 1 lb), peeled and chopped

¾ cup red wine
1 tbsp freshly chopped basil
1 green bell pepper, deseeded and sliced
10 pimiento-stuffed olives, cut in half crossways
salt and freshly ground black pepper
fresh basil leaves, to garnish

For the saffron rice:
1 tbsp olive oil
2 tbsp butter
1 small onion, peeled and finely chopped
few strands of saffron, crushed
1½ cups long-grain white rice
2 cups chicken stock

Preheat the oven to 300˚F. Heat the oil in a large flameproof casserole dish and add the pork in batches. Fry over a high heat until browned. Transfer to a plate until all the pork is browned.

Lower the heat and add the onion to the casserole. Cook for a further 5 minutes, until soft and starting to brown. Add the garlic and stir briefly before returning the pork to the casserole. Add the flour and stir.

Add the tomatoes. Gradually stir in the red wine and add the basil. Bring to simmering point and cover. Transfer the casserole to the lower part of the preheated oven and cook for 1½ hours. Stir in the green pepper and olives and cook for 30 minutes. Season to taste with salt and pepper.

Meanwhile, to make the saffron rice, heat the oil with the butter in a saucepan. Add the onion and cook for 5 minutes over a medium heat until softened. Add the saffron and rice, and stir well. Add the stock, bring to a boil, cover, and reduce the heat as low as possible. Cook for 15 minutes, covered, until the rice is tender and the stock is absorbed. Adjust the seasoning and serve with the stew, garnished with fresh basil.

Try this: FOR AN APPETIZER: 52 FOR DESSERT: 364

Hot Salami & Vegetable Gratin

SERVES 4

6 medium carrots
1½ cups fine green beans
1¾ cups asparagus tips
1 cup frozen peas
8 oz Italian salami
1 tbsp olive oil

1 tbsp freshly chopped mint
2 tbsp butter
1¼ cups baby
　spinach leaves
⅔ cup heavy cream
salt and freshly ground

black pepper
1 small or ½ an olive
　ciabatta loaf
1½ cups Parmesan
　cheese, grated
green salad, to serve

Preheat the oven to 400°F. Peel and slice the carrots, trim the beans and asparagus, and reserve. Cook the carrots in a saucepan of lightly salted, boiling water for 5 minutes. Add the remaining vegetables, except the spinach, and cook for a further 5 minutes, or until tender. Drain and place in an ovenproof dish.

Discard any skin from the outside of the salami, if necessary, then chop roughly. Heat the oil in a skillet and fry the salami for 4–5 minutes, stirring occasionally, until golden. Using a slotted spoon, transfer the salami to the ovenproof dish and scatter over the mint.

Add the butter to the skillet and cook the spinach for 1–2 minutes, or until just wilted. Stir in the heavy cream and season well with salt and pepper. Spoon the mixture over the vegetables.

Whiz the ciabatta loaf in a food processor to make bread crumbs. Stir in the Parmesan cheese and sprinkle over the vegetables. Bake in the preheated oven for 20 minutes, until golden and heated through. Serve with a green salad.

Try this: FOR AN APPETIZER: 50 FOR DESSERT: 350

Antipasto Penne

SERVES 4

3 medium zucchini, trimmed
4 plum tomatoes
6 oz Italian ham
2 tbsp olive oil
salt and freshly ground
    black pepper

12 oz dried penne pasta
10-oz jar antipasto
1 cup mozzarella cheese,
    drained and diced
1 cup Gorgonzola cheese,
    crumbled

3 tbsp freshly chopped
    flat-leaf parsley

Preheat the broiler just before cooking. Cut the zucchini into thick slices. Rinse the tomatoes and cut into quarters, then cut the ham into strips. Pour the oil into a baking dish and place under the broiler for 2 minutes, or until almost smoking. Remove from the broiler and stir in the zucchini. Return to the broiler and cook for 8 minutes, stirring occasionally. Remove from the broiler, add the tomatoes, and cook for a further 3 minutes.

Add the ham to the baking dish and cook under the broiler for 4 minutes, until all the vegetables are charred and the ham is brown. Season to taste with salt and pepper.

Meanwhile, plunge the pasta into a large saucepan of lightly salted, boiling water, return to a rapid boil, stir, and cook for 8 minutes, or until cooked but still firm. Drain well and return to the saucepan.

Stir the antipasto into the vegetables and cook under the broiler for 2 minutes, or until heated through. Add the cooked pasta and toss together gently with the remaining ingredients. Broil for a further 4 minutes, then serve immediately.

Try this: FOR AN APPETIZER: 46   FOR DESSERT: 380

Chorizo with Pasta in a Tomato Sauce

SERVES 4

2 tbsp butter
2 tbsp olive oil
2 large onions, peeled
   and finely sliced
1 tsp brown sugar
2 garlic cloves, peeled
   and crushed

8 oz chorizo, sliced
1 chile pepper, deseeded
   and finely sliced
14-oz can chopped tomatoes
1 tbsp sun-dried
   tomato paste
⅔ cup red wine

salt and freshly ground
   black pepper
1 lb rigatoni
freshly chopped parsley,
   to garnish

Melt the butter with the olive oil in a large heavy-based pan. Add the onions and sugar and cook over a low heat, stirring occasionally, for 15 minutes, or until soft and starting to caramelize.

Add the garlic and chorizo to the pan and cook for 5 minutes. Stir in the chile pepper, chopped tomatoes, and tomato paste, and pour in the wine. Season well with salt and pepper. Bring to a boil, cover, reduce the heat, and simmer for 30 minutes, stirring occasionally. Remove the lid and simmer for a further 10 minutes, or until the sauce starts to thicken.

Meanwhile, bring a large pan of lightly salted water to a rapid boil. Add the pasta and cook according to the package instructions, or until cooked but still firm.

Drain the pasta, reserving 2 tablespoons of the water, and return to the pan. Add the chorizo sauce with the reserved cooking water and toss gently until the pasta is evenly covered. Tip into a warmed serving dish, sprinkle with the parsley, and serve immediately.

Try this: FOR AN APPETIZER: 54   FOR DESSERT: 370

Penne with Artichokes, Bacon & Mushrooms

SERVES 6

2 tbsp olive oil
 oz smoked bacon or
  pancetta, chopped
1 small onion, peeled
  and finely sliced
1¾ cups button mushrooms,
  cleaned and sliced
2 garlic cloves, peeled
  and finely chopped

14-oz can artichoke hearts,
  drained and halved or
  quartered if large
½ cup dry white wine
½ cup chicken stock
3 tbsp heavy cream
1 cup freshly grated
  Parmesan cheese,
  plus extra to serve

salt and freshly
  ground black pepper
1 lb penne
shredded basil leaves,
  to garnish

Heat the olive oil in a frying pan and add the pancetta or bacon and the onion. Cook over a medium heat for 8–10 minutes, or until the bacon is crisp and the onion is just golden. Add the mushrooms and garlic and cook for a further 5 minutes, or until softened.

Add the artichoke hearts to the mushroom mixture and cook for 3–4 minutes. Pour in the wine, bring to a boil, then simmer rapidly until the liquid is reduced and syrupy.

Pour in the chicken stock, bring to a boil, then simmer rapidly for about 5 minutes, or until slightly reduced. Reduce the heat slightly, then slowly stir in the heavy cream and Parmesan cheese. Season the sauce to taste with salt and pepper.

Meanwhile, bring a large pan of lightly salted water to a rapid boil. Add the pasta and cook according to the package instructions, or until cooked but still firm.

Drain the pasta thoroughly and transfer to a large warmed serving dish. Pour over the sauce and toss together. Garnish with shredded basil and serve with extra Parmesan cheese.

Try this: FOR AN APPETIZER: 36   FOR DESSERT: 376

Ham Steak with Red Wine Sauce & Pasta

SERVES 2

2 tbsp butter
⅔ cup red wine
4 red onions, peeled
    and sliced
4 tbsp orange juice

1 tsp brown sugar
8 oz ham steak, trimmed
6 oz fusilli
freshly ground black pepper
    3 tbsp whole-grain

mustard
2 tbsp freshly chopped
    flat-leaf parsley, plus
    sprigs to garnish

Preheat the broiler to a medium heat before cooking. Heat the butter with the red wine in a large heavy-based pan. Add the onions, cover with a tight fitting lid, and cook over a low heat for 30 minutes, or until softened and transparent. Remove the lid from the pan, stir in the orange juice and sugar, then increase the heat and cook for about 10 minutes, until the onions are golden.

Meanwhile cook the ham steak under the preheated broiler, turning at least once, for 4–6 minutes, or until tender. Cut the cooked ham into bite-sized pieces. Reserve and keep warm.

Meanwhile, bring a large pan of lightly salted water to a rapid boil. Add the pasta and cook according to the package instructions, or until cooked but still firm. Drain the pasta thoroughly, return to the pan, season with a little pepper, and keep warm.

Stir the whole-grain mustard and chopped parsley into the onion sauce, then pour over the pasta. Add the ham pieces to the pan and toss lightly to thoroughly coat the pasta with the sauce. Pile the pasta mixture onto two warmed serving plates. Garnish with sprigs of flat-leaf parsley and serve immediately.

Try this: FOR AN APPETIZER: 26   FOR DESSERT: 358

Speedy Pork with Yellow Bean Sauce

SERVES 4

1 lb pork fillet
2 tbsp light soy sauce
2 tbsp orange juice
2 tsp cornstarch
3 tbsp peanut oil
2 garlic cloves,

peeled and crushed
2 medium carrots, peeled
    and cut into matchsticks
1 cup fine green beans,
    trimmed and halved
2 green onions, trimmed

and cut into strips
4 tbsp yellow bean sauce
1 tbsp freshly chopped
    flat-leaf parsley, to garnish
freshly cooked egg noodles,
    to serve

Remove any fat or sinew from the pork fillet, and cut into thin strips. Blend the soy sauce, orange juice, and cornstarch in a bowl and mix thoroughly. Place the meat in a shallow dish, pour over the soy sauce mixture, cover, and let marinate in the refrigerator for 1 hour. Drain with a slotted spoon, reserving the marinade.

Heat the wok, then add 2 tablespoons of the oil and stir-fry the pork with the garlic for 2 minutes, or until the meat is sealed. Remove with a slotted spoon and reserve.

Add the remaining oil to the wok and cook the carrots, beans, and green onions for 3 minutes, until tender but still crisp. Return the pork to the wok with the reserved marinade, then pour over the yellow bean sauce. Stir-fry for a further 1–2 minutes, or until the pork is tender. Sprinkle with the chopped parsley and serve immediately with freshly cooked egg noodles.

Pork Chop Hot Pot

SERVES 4

4 pork chops
flour for dusting
8–12 medium shallots
    (about 8 oz), peeled
2 garlic cloves, peeled
20 sun-dried tomatoes
2 tbsp olive oil

14-oz can plum tomatoes
⅔ cup red wine
⅔ cup chicken stock
3 tbsp tomato paste
2 tbsp freshly chopped
    oregano
salt and freshly ground

black pepper
fresh oregano leaves,
    to garnish

To serve:
freshly cooked new potatoes
snap beans

Preheat the oven to 375°F, 10 minutes before cooking. Trim the pork chops, removing any excess fat, wipe with a clean, damp cloth, then dust with a little flour and reserve. Cut the shallots in half if large. Chop the garlic and slice the sun-dried tomatoes.

Heat the olive oil in a large casserole dish and cook the pork chops for about 5 minutes, turning occasionally during cooking, until browned all over. Using a slotted spoon, carefully lift out of the dish and reserve. Add the shallots and cook for 5 minutes, stirring occasionally.

Return the pork chops to the casserole dish and scatter with the garlic and sun-dried tomatoes, then pour over the can of tomatoes with their juices.

Blend the red wine, stock, and tomato paste together and add the chopped oregano. Season to taste with salt and pepper, then pour over the pork chops and bring to a gentle boil. Cover with a close-fitting lid and cook in the preheated oven for 1 hour, or until the pork chops are tender. Adjust the seasoning to taste, then scatter with a few oregano leaves and serve immediately with freshly cooked potatoes and snap beans.

Try this: FOR AN APPETIZER: 34 FOR DESSERT: 368

Pork Fried Noodles

SERVES 4

4 oz dried thread
  egg noodles
½ cup broccoli florets
4 tbsp peanut oil
12 oz pork tenderloin, cut
  into slices
3 tbsp soy sauce
1 tbsp lemon juice
pinch of sugar

1 tsp chili sauce
1 tbsp sesame oil
1-inch piece fresh ginger,
  peeled and cut into sticks
1 garlic clove, peeled
  and chopped
1 green chile pepper,
  deseeded and sliced
1½ cups snow peas, halved

2 medium eggs,
  lightly beaten
8-oz can water chestnuts,
  drained and sliced

To garnish:
radish rose
green onion tassels

Place the noodles in a bowl and cover with boiling water. Let stand for 20 minutes, stirring occasionally, or until tender. Drain and reserve. Meanwhile, blanch the broccoli in a saucepan of lightly salted boiling water for 2 minutes. Drain, refresh under cold running water, and reserve.

Heat a large wok or skillet, add the peanut oil, and heat until just smoking. Add the pork and stir-fry for 5 minutes, or until browned. Using a slotted spoon, remove the pork slices and reserve.

Mix together the soy sauce, lemon juice, sugar, chile sauce, and sesame oil and reserve.

Add the ginger to the wok and stir-fry for 30 seconds. Add the garlic and chile and stir-fry for 30 seconds. Add the reserved broccoli and stir-fry for 3 minutes. Stir in the snow peas, pork, and reserved noodles with the beaten eggs and water chestnuts, and stir-fry for 5 minutes, or until heated through. Pour over the reserved chile sauce, toss well, and turn into a warmed serving dish. Garnish and serve immediately.

Try this: FOR AN APPETIZER: 34   FOR DESSERT: 374

Hoisin Pork

SERVES 4

3-lb piece lean belly
   pork, boned
sea salt
2 tsp Chinese five spice

powder
2 garlic cloves, peeled
   and chopped
1 tsp sesame oil

4 tbsp hoisin sauce
1 tbsp clear honey
assorted lettuce leaves,
   to garnish

Preheat the oven to 400°F, 15 minutes before cooking. Using a sharp knife, cut the pork skin in a crisscross pattern, making sure not to cut all the way through into the flesh. Rub the salt evenly over the skin and let stand for 30 minutes.

Meanwhile, mix together the five spice powder, garlic, sesame oil, hoisin sauce, and honey until smooth. Rub the mixture evenly over the pork skin. Place the pork on a plate and chill in the refrigerator to marinate for up to 6 hours.

Place the pork on a wire rack set inside a roasting pan and roast the pork in the preheated oven for 1–1¼ hours, or until the pork is crisp and the juices run clear when pierced with a skewer.

Remove the pork from the heat, let it rest for 15 minutes, then cut into strips. Arrange on a warmed serving platter. Garnish with lettuce leaves and serve immediately.

Try this: FOR AN APPETIZER: 40   FOR DESSERT: 320

Pork with Black Bean Sauce

SERVES 4

1½ lb pork tenderloin
4 tbsp light soy sauce
2 tbsp peanut oil
1 garlic clove, peeled
  and chopped
1-inch piece fresh ginger,
  peeled and cut into

matchsticks
1 large carrot, peeled
  and sliced
1 red bell pepper, deseeded
  and sliced
1 green bell pepper,
  deseeded and sliced

5½-oz jar black bean sauce
salt
snipped fresh chives,
  to garnish
freshly steamed rice,
  to serve

Using a sharp knife, trim the pork, discarding any fat or sinew, and cut into bite-sized chunks. Place in a large shallow dish and spoon over the soy sauce. Turn to coat evenly, cover with plastic wrap, and let marinate for at least 30 minutes in the refrigerator. When ready to use, lift the pork from the marinade, shaking off as much marinade as possible, and pat dry with a paper towel. Reserve the marinade.

Heat a wok and add the peanut oil; when hot, add the chopped garlic and ginger, and stir-fry for 30 seconds. Add the carrot and the red and green peppers and stir-fry for 3–4 minutes, or until just softened.

Add the pork to the wok and stir-fry for 5–7 minutes, or until browned all over and tender. Pour in the reserved marinade and black bean sauce. Bring to a boil, stirring constantly until well blended, then simmer for 1 minute, until heated through thoroughly. Tip into a warmed serving dish or spoon onto individual plates. Garnish with snipped chives and serve immediately with steamed rice.

Try this: FOR AN APPETIZER: 58   FOR DESSERT: 380

Italian Risotto

SERVES 4

1 onion, peeled
2 garlic cloves, peeled
1 tbsp olive oil
4 oz Italian salami
   or speck, chopped
1 cup asparagus
1¾ cups risotto rice

⅔ cup dry white wine
4¼ cups chicken stock,
   warmed
1 cup frozen fava beans,
   defrosted
1 cup Dolcelatte or
   Gorgonzola cheese, diced

3 tbsp freshly chopped
   mixed herbs, such as
   parsley and basil
salt and freshly ground
   black pepper

Chop the onion and garlic and reserve. Heat the olive oil in a large skillet and cook the salami for 3–5 minutes, or until golden. Using a slotted spoon, transfer to a plate, and keep warm. Add the asparagus and stir-fry for 2–3 minutes, until just wilted. Transfer to the plate with the salami. Add the onion and garlic, and cook for 5 minutes, or until softened.

Add the rice to the pan and cook for about 2 minutes. Add the wine, bring to a boil, then simmer, stirring until the wine has been absorbed. Add half the stock and return to a boil. Simmer, stirring until the liquid has been absorbed.

Add half of the remaining stock and the fava beans to the rice mixture. Bring to a boil, then simmer for a further 5–10 minutes, or until all of the liquid has been absorbed.

Add the remaining stock, bring to a boil, then simmer until all the liquid is absorbed and the rice is tender. Stir in the remaining ingredients until the cheese has just melted. Serve immediately.

Lamb Pilaf

SERVES 4

2 tbsp vegetable oil
¼ cup flaked or
   slivered almonds
1 medium onion, peeled
   and finely chopped
1 medium carrot, peeled
   and finely chopped
1 celery stalk, trimmed
   and finely chopped
12 oz lean lamb,

cut into chunks
¼ tsp ground cinnamon
¼ tsp chile pepper flakes
2 large tomatoes, skinned,
   deseeded and chopped
grated rind of 1 orange
1¾ cups easy-cook
   brown basmati rice
2 cups vegetable
   or lamb stock

2 tbsp freshly
   snipped chives
3 tbsp freshly
   chopped cilantro
salt and freshly ground
   black pepper

To garnish:
lemon slices
sprigs of fresh cilantro

Preheat the oven to 275°F. Heat the oil in a flameproof casserole with a tight-fitting lid and add the almonds. Cook for about 1 minute until just starting to brown, stirring often. Add the onion, carrot, and celery, and cook gently for a further 8–10 minutes until soft and lightly browned.

Increase the heat and add the lamb. Cook for a further 5 minutes until the lamb has changed color. Add the ground cinnamon and chile pepper flakes, and stir briefly before adding the tomatoes and orange rind.

Stir and add the rice, then the stock. Bring slowly to a boil and cover tightly. Transfer to the preheated oven and cook for 30–35 minutes, until the rice is tender and the stock is absorbed.

Remove from the oven and let stand for 5 minutes before stirring in the chives and cilantro. Season to taste with salt and pepper. Garnish with the lemon slices and sprigs of fresh cilantro and serve immediately.

Try this: FOR AN APPETIZER: 20   FOR DESSERT: 352

Lancashire Hot Pot

SERVES 4

2¼ lb lamb cutlets
2 tbsp vegetable oil
2 large onions,
   peeled and sliced
2 tsp all-purpose flour
⅔ cup vegetable
   or lamb stock

4–5 medium waxy potatoes
   (about 1½ lb), peeled and
   thickly sliced
salt and freshly ground
   black pepper
1 bay leaf
2 sprigs of fresh thyme

1 tbsp melted butter
2 tbsp freshly chopped
   herbs, to garnish
freshly cooked green beans,
   to serve

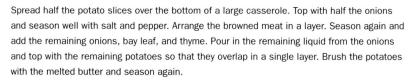

Preheat the oven to 325°F. Trim any excess fat from the lamb cutlets. Heat the oil in a skillet and brown the cutlets in batches for 3–4 minutes. Remove with a slotted spoon and reserve. Add the onions to the skillet and cook for 6–8 minutes, until softened and just beginning to color, then remove and reserve.

Stir in the flour and cook for a few seconds, then gradually pour in the stock, stirring well, and bring to a boil. Remove from the heat.

Spread half the potato slices over the bottom of a large casserole. Top with half the onions and season well with salt and pepper. Arrange the browned meat in a layer. Season again and add the remaining onions, bay leaf, and thyme. Pour in the remaining liquid from the onions and top with the remaining potatoes so that they overlap in a single layer. Brush the potatoes with the melted butter and season again.

Cover the saucepan and cook in the preheated oven for 2 hours, uncovering for the last 30 minutes to allow the potatoes to brown. Garnish with chopped herbs and serve immediately with green beans.

Try this: FOR AN APPETIZER: 38   FOR DESSERT: 366

Marinated Lamb Chops with Garlic Fried Potatoes

SERVES 4

4 thick lamb chump chops
3 tbsp olive oil
4 medium potatoes (about
   1¼ lb), peeled and cut into
   ½-inch dice
6 unpeeled garlic cloves
mixed lettuce or freshly

cooked vegetables,
   to serve

For the marinade:
1 small bunch of fresh
   thyme, leaves removed
1 tbsp freshly

chopped rosemary
1 tsp salt
2 garlic cloves, peeled
   and crushed
rind and juice of 1 lemon
2 tbsp olive oil

Trim the chops of any excess fat, wipe with a clean damp cloth, and reserve. To make the marinade, using a pestle and mortar, pound the thyme leaves and rosemary with the salt until pulpy. Add the garlic and continue pounding until crushed. Stir in the lemon rind and juice and the olive oil.

Pour the marinade over the lamb chops, turning them until they are well coated. Cover lightly and let marinate in the refrigerator for about 1 hour.

Meanwhile, heat the oil in a large nonstick skillet. Add the potatoes and garlic and cook over a low heat for about 20 minutes, stirring occasionally. Increase the heat and cook for a further 10–15 minutes, until golden. Drain on a paper towel and add salt to taste. Keep warm.

Heat a griddle pan until almost smoking. Add the lamb chops and cook for 3–4 minutes on each side, until golden but still pink in the middle. Serve with the potatoes, and either a mixed salad or freshly cooked vegetables.

Try this: FOR AN APPETIZER: 62   FOR DESSERT: 362

Roasted Lamb
with Rosemary & Garlic

SERVES 6

3½ lb leg of lamb
8 garlic cloves, peeled
few sprigs of fresh rosemary
salt and freshly ground
   black pepper

4 slices pancetta
4 tbsp olive oil
4 tbsp red wine vinegar
6 medium potatoes
   (about 2 lb)

1 large onion
sprigs of fresh rosemary,
   to garnish
freshly cooked ratatouille,
   to serve

Preheat the oven to 400°F, 15 minutes before roasting. Wipe the leg of lamb with a clean damp cloth, then place the lamb in a large roasting pan. With a sharp knife, make small, deep incisions into the meat. Cut 2–3 garlic cloves into small slivers, then insert with a few small sprigs of rosemary into the lamb. Season to taste with salt and pepper and cover the lamb with the slices of pancetta.

Drizzle over 1 tablespoon of the olive oil and lay a few more rosemary sprigs across the lamb. Roast in the preheated oven for 30 minutes, then pour over the vinegar.

Peel the potatoes and cut into large dice. Peel the onion and cut into thick wedges, then thickly slice the remaining garlic. Arrange around the lamb. Pour the remaining olive oil over the potatoes, then reduce the oven temperature to 350°F and roast for a further 1 hour, or until the lamb is tender. Garnish with fresh sprigs of rosemary and serve immediately with the roast potatoes and ratatouille.

Try this: FOR AN APPETIZER: 60   FOR DESSERT: 358

Braised Lamb with Fava Beans

SERVES 4

1½ lb lamb, cut into large
   chunks
1 tbsp all-purpose flour
1 onion
2 garlic cloves
1 tbsp olive oil
14-oz can chopped tomatoes

with basil
1¼ cups lamb stock
2 tbsp freshly chopped
   thyme
2 tbsp freshly chopped
   oregano
salt and freshly ground black

pepper
1¼ cups frozen
   fava beans
fresh oregano,
   to garnish
creamy mashed potatoes,
   to serve

Trim the lamb, discarding any fat or gristle, then place the flour in a plastic bag, add the lamb, and toss until coated thoroughly. Peel and slice the onion and garlic and reserve. Heat the olive oil in a heavy-based saucepan and when hot, add the lamb and cook, stirring until the meat is sealed and browned all over. Using a slotted spoon, transfer the lamb to a plate and reserve.

Add the onion and garlic to the saucepan and cook for 3 minutes, stirring frequently until softened, then return the lamb to the saucepan. Add the chopped tomatoes with their juices, the stock, and the chopped thyme and oregano to the pan, and season to taste with salt and pepper. Bring to a boil, then cover with a close-fitting lid, reduce the heat, and simmer for 1 hour.

Add the fava beans to the lamb and simmer for 20–30 minutes, or until the lamb is tender. Garnish with fresh oregano and serve with creamy mashed potatoes.

Try this: FOR AN APPETIZER: 30 FOR DESSERT: 376

Spaghetti Bolognese

SERVES 4

1 carrot
2 celery stalks
1 onion
2 garlic cloves
1 lb lean ground
   beef steak
8 oz smoked streaky bacon,

   chopped
1 tbsp all-purpose flour
⅔ cup red wine
13-oz can chopped tomatoes
2 tbsp tomato paste
2 tsp dried mixed herbs
salt and freshly ground

   black pepper
pinch of sugar
12 oz spaghetti
sprigs of fresh oregano,
   to garnish
shavings of Parmesan
   cheese, to serve

Peel and chop the carrot, trim and chop the celery, then peel and chop the onion and garlic. Heat a large nonstick skillet and fry the beef and bacon for 5–10 minutes, stirring occasionally, until browned. Add the prepared vegetables to the skillet and cook for about 3 minutes, or until softened, stirring occasionally.

Add the flour and cook for 1 minute. Stir in the red wine, tomatoes, tomato paste, mixed herbs, and sugar, and season to taste. Bring to a boil, then cover and simmer for 45 minutes, stirring occasionally.

Meanwhile, bring a large saucepan of lightly salted water to a rapid boil and cook the spaghetti according to package directions, or until cooked but still firm. Drain well and divide between four serving plates. Spoon over the sauce, garnish with a few sprigs of oregano, and serve immediately with plenty of Parmesan shavings.

Try this: FOR AN APPETIZER: 56   FOR DESSERT: 372

Lasagne

SERVES 4

6 tbsp butter
4 tbsp all-purpose flour
3 cups milk
1 tsp whole-grain mustard
salt and freshly ground
   black pepper

¼ tsp freshly
   grated nutmeg
9 sheets lasagne
1 quantity of prepared
   Bolognese sauce
1½ cups freshly grated

Parmesan cheese
freshly chopped parsley,
   to garnish
garlic bread,
   to serve

Preheat the oven to 400°F, 15 minutes before cooking. Melt the butter in a small heavy-based pan, add the flour, and cook gently, stirring, for 2 minutes. Remove from the heat and gradually stir in the milk. Return to the heat and cook, stirring, for 2 minutes, or until the sauce thickens. Bring to a boil, remove from the heat, and stir in the mustard. Season to taste with salt, pepper, and nutmeg.

Butter a rectangular ovenproof dish and spread a thin layer of the white sauce over the base. Cover completely with three sheets of lasagne.

Spoon one-quarter of the prepared Bolognese sauce over the lasagne. Spoon over one-quarter of the remaining white sauce, then sprinkle with one-quarter of the grated Parmesan cheese. Repeat the layers, finishing with Parmesan cheese.

Bake in the preheated oven for 30 minutes, or until golden brown. Garnish with chopped parsley and serve immediately with warm garlic bread.

Try this: FOR AN APPETIZER: 50   FOR DESSERT: 370

Italian Beef Pot Roast

SERVES 6

4 lb brisket of beef
3 small onions, peeled
3 garlic cloves, peeled
    and chopped
2 celery sticks, trimmed
    and chopped
2 carrots, peeled and sliced
3–4 medium tomatoes

(about 1 lb)
1¼ cups Italian
    red wine
2 tbsp olive oil
1¼ cups beef stock
1 tbsp tomato paste
2 tsp freeze-dried
    mixed herbs

salt and freshly ground
    black pepper
2 tbsp butter
¼ cup all-purpose flour
freshly cooked vegetables,
    to serve

Place the beef in a bowl. Add the onions, garlic, celery, and carrots. Place the tomatoes in a bowl and cover with boiling water. Let stand for 2 minutes and drain. Peel away the skins, discard the seeds, and chop, then add to the bowl with the red wine. Cover and marinate in the refrigerator overnight.

Lift the marinated beef from the bowl and pat dry with a paper towel. Heat the olive oil in a large casserole dish and cook the beef until it is browned all over, then remove from the dish. Drain the vegetables from the marinade, reserving the marinade. Add the vegetables to the casserole dish and fry gently for 5 minutes, stirring occasionally, until all the vegetables are browned.

Preheat the oven to 300° F. Return the beef to the casserole dish with the marinade, beef stock, tomato paste, and mixed herbs, and season with salt and pepper. Bring to a boil, then cover and cook in the preheated oven for 3 hours.

Using a slotted spoon, transfer the beef and any large vegetables to a plate and let stand in a warm place. Blend the butter and flour to form a paste. Bring the casserole juices to a boil, then gradually stir in small spoonfuls of the paste. Cook until thickened. Serve with the sauce and a selection of vegetables.

Try this: FOR AN APPETIZER: 18   FOR DESSERT: 350

Steaks with Tomato & Garlic Sauce

SERVES 4

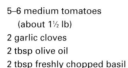

5–6 medium tomatoes
(about 1½ lb)
2 garlic cloves
2 tbsp olive oil
2 tbsp freshly chopped basil

2 tbsp freshly
chopped oregano
2 tbsp red wine
salt and freshly ground
black pepper

15 large, pitted black olives,
chopped
4 x 6 oz tenderloin steaks
freshly cooked vegetables,
to serve

Make a small cross on the top of each tomato and place in a large bowl. Cover with boiling water and let stand for 2 minutes. Using a slotted spoon, remove the tomatoes and skin carefully. Repeat until all the tomatoes are skinned. Place on a cutting board, cut into quarters, remove the seeds, and roughly chop, then reserve.

Peel and chop the garlic. Heat half the olive oil in a saucepan and cook the garlic for 30 seconds. Add the chopped tomatoes with the basil, oregano, and red wine, and season to taste with salt and pepper. Bring to a boil, then reduce the heat, cover, and simmer for 15 minutes, stirring occasionally, or until the sauce is reduced and thickened. Stir the olives into the sauce and keep warm while cooking the steaks.

Meanwhile, lightly oil a griddle pan or heavy-based skillet with the remaining olive oil and cook the steaks for 2 minutes on each side to seal. Continue to cook the steaks for a further 2–4 minutes, depending on personal preference. Serve the steaks immediately with the garlic sauce and freshly cooked vegetables.

Try this: FOR AN APPETIZER: 34   FOR DESSERT: 354

Spicy Beef Chili

SERVES 4

2 tbsp olive oil
1 onion, peeled and
    finely chopped
1 red bell pepper, deseeded
    and sliced
1 lb ground beef steak
2 garlic cloves, peeled
    and crushed

2 red chile peppers,
    deseeded and finely sliced
salt and freshly ground
    black pepper
14-oz can chopped tomatoes
2 tbsp tomato paste
14-oz can red kidney
    beans, drained

2 squares baking chocolate,
    grated
12 oz dried fusilli
knob of butter
2 tbsp freshly chopped
    flat-leaf parsley
paprika, to garnish
sour cream, to serve

Heat the olive oil in a large, heavy-based pan. Add the onion and red pepper and cook for 5 minutes, or until beginning to soften. Add the minced beef and cook over a high heat for another 5–8 minutes, or until the meat is browned. Stir with a wooden spoon during cooking to break up any lumps in the meat. Add the garlic and chile pepper, fry for 1 minute, then season to taste with salt and pepper.

Add the chopped tomatoes, tomato paste, and the kidney beans to the pan. Bring to a boil, lower the heat, and simmer, covered, for at least 40 minutes, stirring occasionally. Stir in the grated chocolate and cook for 3 minutes, or until melted.

Meanwhile, bring a large pan of lightly salted water to a rapid boil. Add the fusilli and cook according to the package instructions, or until cooked but still firm.

Drain the pasta, return to the pan, and toss with the butter and parsley. Tip into a warmed serving dish or spoon onto individual plates. Spoon the sauce over the pasta. Sprinkle with paprika and serve immediately with spoonfuls of sour cream.

Try this: FOR AN APPETIZER: 48   FOR DESSERT: 362

Sweet & Sour Shredded Beef

SERVES 4

12 oz sirloin steak
1 tsp sesame oil
2 tbsp Chinese rice wine
   or sweet sherry
2 tbsp dark soy sauce
1 tsp cornstarch
4 tbsp pineapple juice
2 tsp light brown sugar

1 tsp sherry vinegar
salt and freshly ground
   black pepper
2 tbsp peanut oil
2 medium carrots, peeled
   and cut into matchsticks
1½ cups snow peas, trimmed
   and cut into matchsticks

1 bunch green onions,
   trimmed and shredded
2 garlic cloves, peeled
   and crushed
1 tbsp toasted sesame seeds
freshly cooked Thai fragrant
   rice, to serve

Cut the steak across the grain into thin strips. Put in a bowl with the sesame oil, 1 tablespoon of the Chinese rice wine or sherry, and 1 tablespoon of the soy sauce. Mix well, cover, and let marinate in the refrigerator for 30 minutes.

In a small bowl, blend together the cornstarch with the remaining Chinese rice wine or sherry, then stir in the pineapple juice, remaining soy sauce, sugar, and vinegar. Season with a little salt and pepper and reserve.

Heat a wok until hot, add 1 tablespoon of the oil, then drain the beef, reserving the marinade, and stir-fry for 1–2 minutes, or until browned. Remove from the wok and reserve.

Add the remaining oil to the wok, then add the carrots and stir-fry for 1 minute. Add the snow peas and green onions and stir-fry for a further 1 minute.

Return the beef to the wok with the sauce, reserved marinade, and garlic. Continue cooking for 1 minute, or until the vegetables are tender and the sauce is bubbling. Turn the stir-fry into a warmed serving dish, sprinkle with toasted sesame seeds, and serve immediately with the Thai fragrant rice.

Try this: FOR AN APPETIZER: 52   FOR DESSERT: 368

Red Chicken Curry

SERVES 4

1 cup coconut milk
2 tbsp vegetable oil
2 garlic cloves, peeled and
   finely chopped
2 tbsp Thai red curry paste
2 tbsp Thai fish sauce

2 tsp sugar
12 oz boneless, skinless
   chicken breast,
   finely sliced
2 cups chicken stock
2 lime leaves, shredded

(optional)
chopped red chile pepper,
   to garnish
freshly boiled rice or
   steamed Thai fragrant
   rice, to serve

Pour the coconut milk into a small saucepan and heat gently. Meanwhile, heat a wok or large skillet and add the oil. When the oil is hot, swirl the oil around the wok until it is lightly coated, then add the garlic and stir-fry for 10–20 seconds, or until the garlic begins to brown. Add the curry paste and stir-fry for a few more seconds, then pour in the warmed coconut milk.

Cook the coconut-milk mixture for 5 minutes, or until the milk has curdled and thickened. Stir in the fish sauce and sugar. Add the finely sliced chicken breast and cook for 3–4 minutes, or until the chicken has turned white.

Pour the stock into the wok, bring to a boil, then simmer for 1–2 minutes, or until the chicken is cooked through. Stir in the shredded lime leaves. Turn into a warmed serving dish, garnish with chopped red chile pepper, and serve immediately with rice.

Try this: FOR AN APPETIZER: 54   FOR DESSERT: 374

Braised Chicken in Beer

SERVES 4

4 chicken joints, skinned
¾ cup pitted dried prunes
2 bay leaves
12 shallots
2 tsp olive oil
1¾ cups small button
   mushrooms, cleaned
1 tsp dark brown sugar

½ tsp whole-grain mustard
2 tsp tomato paste
⅔ cup pint beer
⅔ cup chicken stock
salt and freshly ground
   black pepper
2 tsp cornstarch
2 tsp lemon juice

2 tbsp chopped fresh parsley
flat-leaf parsley, to garnish

To serve:
mashed potatoes
seasonal green vegetables

Preheat the oven to 325˚F. Cut each chicken joint in half and put in an ovenproof casserole with the prunes and bay leaves.

To peel the shallots, put in a small bowl and cover with boiling water. Drain the shallots after 2 minutes and rinse under cold water until cool enough to handle. The skins should then peel away easily. Heat the oil in a large nonstick skillet. Add the shallots and gently cook for about 5 minutes, until they begin to color.

Add the mushrooms to the skillet and cook for a further 3–4 minutes, until both the mushrooms and onions are softened. Sprinkle the sugar over the shallots and mushrooms, then add the mustard, tomato paste, beer, and chicken stock. Season to taste with salt and pepper and bring to a boil, stirring to combine. Carefully pour over the chicken. Cover the casserole and cook in the preheated oven for 1 hour. Blend the cornstarch with the lemon juice and 1 tablespoon of cold water and stir into the chicken casserole. Return the casserole to the oven for 10 minutes, or until the chicken is cooked and the vegetables are tender.

Remove the bay leaves and stir in the chopped parsley. Garnish the chicken with the flat-leaf parsley. Serve with the mashed potatoes and fresh green vegetables.

Try this: FOR AN APPETIZER: 22   FOR DESSERT: 376

Chicken Baked in a Salt Crust

SERVES 4

4 lb chicken
salt and black pepper
1 medium onion, peeled
sprig of fresh rosemary
sprig of fresh thyme
1 bay leaf
1 tbsp butter, softened

1 garlic clove, peeled
    and crushed
pinch of ground paprika
finely grated rind of ½ lemon

To garnish:
fresh herbs, lemon slices

For the salt crust:
8 cups all-purpose flour
1½ cups fine cooking salt
1½ cups coarse sea salt
2 tbsp oil

Preheat the oven to 325°F. Remove the giblets if necessary and rinse the chicken with cold water. Sprinkle the inside with salt and pepper. Put the onion inside with the rosemary, thyme, and bay leaf.

Mix the butter, garlic, paprika, and lemon rind together. Starting at the neck end, gently ease the skin from the chicken and push the mixture under.

To make the salt crust, put the flour and salts in a large mixing bowl and stir together. Make a well in the center. Pour in 2½ cups of cold water and the oil. Mix to a stiff dough, then knead on a lightly floured surface for 2–3 minutes. Roll out the pastry to a circle with a diameter of about 20 inches. Place the chicken, breast-side down, in the middle. Lightly brush the edges with water, then fold over to enclose. Pinch the joints together to seal.

Put the chicken join side down in a roasting pan and cook in the preheated oven for 2¾ hours. Remove from the oven and let stand for 20 minutes.

Break open the hard crust and remove the chicken. Discard the crust. Remove the skin from the chicken, garnish with the fresh herbs and lemon slices. Serve the chicken immediately.

Try this: FOR AN APPETIZER: 48   FOR DESSERT: 356

Slow Roast Chicken with Potatoes & Oregano

SERVES 6

3–4 lb chicken, preferably free range
1 lemon, halved
1 onion, peeled and quartered
4 tbsp butter, softened

salt and freshly ground black pepper
3–4 medium potatoes (about 2¼ lb), peeled and quartered
3–4 tbsp extra-virgin olive oil

1 tbsp dried oregano, crumbled
1 tsp fresh thyme leaves
2 tbsp freshly chopped thyme
fresh sage leaves, to garnish

Preheat the oven to 400°F. Rinse the chicken and dry well, inside and out, with a paper towel. Rub the chicken all over with the lemon halves, then squeeze the juice over it and into the cavity. Put the squeezed halves into the cavity with the quartered onion.

Rub the softened butter all over the chicken and season to taste with salt and pepper, then put it in a large roasting pan, breast-side down. Toss the potatoes in the oil, season with salt and pepper to taste, and add the dried oregano and fresh thyme. Arrange the potatoes with the oil around the chicken and carefully pour ⅔ cup of water into one end of the pan (not over the oil).

Roast in the preheated oven for 25 minutes. Reduce the oven temperature to 375°F and turn the chicken breast-side up. Turn the potatoes, sprinkle over half the fresh herbs, and baste the chicken and potatoes with the juices. Continue roasting for 1 hour, or until the chicken is cooked, basting occasionally. If the liquid evaporates completely, add a little more water. The chicken is done when the juices run clear when the thigh is pierced with a skewer.

Transfer the chicken to a carving board and let it rest for 5 minutes, covered with foil. Return the potatoes to the oven while the chicken is resting. Carve the chicken into serving pieces and arrange on a large heatproof serving dish. Arrange the potatoes around the chicken and drizzle over any remaining juices. Sprinkle with the remaining herbs and serve.

Try this: FOR AN APPETIZER: 62   FOR DESSERT: 378

Lemon Chicken with Potatoes, Rosemary & Olives

SERVES 6

12 skinless boneless
   chicken thighs
1 large lemon
½ cup extra-virgin olive oil
6 garlic cloves,
   peeled and sliced
2 onions, peeled and
   thinly sliced
bunch of fresh rosemary
7–8 medium potatoes (about
   2½ lb), peeled and cut into
   1½-inch pieces
salt and freshly ground
   black pepper

18–24 black pitted olives

To serve:
steamed carrots
zucchini

Preheat the oven to 400°F, 15 minutes before cooking. Trim the chicken thighs and place in a shallow baking dish large enough to hold them in a single layer. Remove the rind from the lemon with a zester or if using a vegetable peeler cut into thin julienne strips. Reserve half and add the remainder to the chicken. Squeeze the lemon juice over the chicken, toss to coat well, and let stand for 10 minutes.

Transfer the chicken to a roasting pan. Add the remaining lemon zest or julienne strips, olive oil, garlic, onions, and half of the rosemary sprigs. Toss gently and let stand for 20 minutes.

Cover the potatoes with lightly salted water and bring to a boil. Cook for 2 minutes, then drain well and add to the chicken. Season to taste with salt and pepper.

Roast the chicken in the preheated oven for 50 minutes, turning frequently and basting, or until the chicken is cooked. Just before the end of cooking time, discard the rosemary and add fresh sprigs of rosemary. Add the olives and stir. Serve immediately with steamed carrots and zucchini.

    Try this: FOR AN APPETIZER: 52 FOR DESSERT: 352

Chicken Parcels with Zucchini & Pasta

SERVES 4

2 tbsp olive oil
4 oz farfalle pasta
1 onion, peeled and
    thinly sliced
1 garlic clove, peeled
    and finely chopped

2 medium zucchini, trimmed
    and thinly sliced
salt and freshly ground
    black pepper
2 tbsp freshly
    chopped oregano

4 plum tomatoes, deseeded
    and coarsely chopped
4 x 6 oz boneless, skinless
    chicken breasts
⅔ cup Italian white wine

Preheat the oven to 400°F, 15 minutes before cooking. Lightly brush four large sheets of nonstick baking parchment with half the oil. Bring a saucepan of lightly salted water to a rapid boil and cook the pasta for 10 minutes, or until cooked but still firm. Drain and reserve.

Heat the remaining oil in a skillet and cook the onion for 2–3 minutes. Add the garlic and cook for 1 minute. Add the zucchini and cook for 1 minute, then remove from the heat, season to taste with salt and pepper, and add half the oregano.

Divide the cooked pasta equally between the 4 sheets of baking parchment, positioning the pasta in the center. Top the pasta with equal amounts of the vegetable mixture, and sprinkle one-quarter of the chopped tomatoes over each.

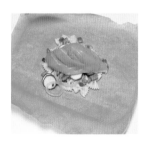

Score the surface of each chicken breast about ½ inch deep. Place a chicken breast on top of the pasta and sprinkle each with the remaining oregano and the white wine. Fold the edges of the paper along the top, then along each side, creating a sealed envelope.

Bake in the preheated oven for 30–35 minutes, or until cooked. Serve immediately.

Try this: FOR AN APPETIZER: 46   FOR DESSERT: 372

Thai Chicken Fried Rice

SERVES 4

6 oz boneless chicken breast
2 tbsp vegetable oil
2 garlic cloves, peeled
   and finely chopped
2 tsp medium curry paste
2¼ cups cold cooked rice

1 tbsp light soy sauce
2 tbsp Thai fish sauce
large pinch of sugar
freshly ground black pepper

To garnish:
2 green onions, trimmed
   and shredded lengthways
½ small onion, peeled
   and finely sliced

Using a sharp knife, trim the chicken, discarding any sinew or fat and cut into small cubes. Reserve.

Heat a wok or large skillet and add the oil when hot, add the garlic and cook for 10–20 seconds, or until just golden. Add the curry paste and stir-fry for a few seconds. Add the chicken and stir-fry for 3–4 minutes, or until tender and the chicken has turned white.

Stir the cold cooked rice into the chicken mixture, then add the soy sauce, fish sauce, and sugar, stirring well after each addition. Stir-fry for 2–3 minutes, or until the chicken is cooked through and the rice is piping hot.

Check the seasoning and, if necessary, add a little extra soy sauce. Turn the rice and chicken mixture into a warmed serving dish. Season lightly with black pepper and garnish with shredded green onion and onion slices. Serve immediately.

Try this: FOR AN APPETIZER: 30 FOR DESSERT: 364

Cheesy Baked
Chicken Macaroni

SERVES 4

1 tbsp olive oil
12 oz boneless and skinless
   chicken breast, diced
3 oz pancetta, diced
1 onion, peeled
   and chopped
1 garlic clove, peeled
   and chopped

12-oz package fresh
   tomato sauce
14-oz can chopped tomatoes
2 tbsp freshly chopped basil,
   plus leaves to garnish
salt and freshly ground
   black pepper
12 oz macaroni

1¼ cups mozzarella cheese,
   drained and chopped
½ cup Gruyère cheese,
   grated
1 cup freshly grated
   Parmesan cheese

Preheat the broiler just before cooking. Heat the oil in large skillet and cook the chicken for 8 minutes, or until browned, stirring occasionally. Drain on a paper towel and reserve. Add the pancetta slices to the skillet and fry on both sides until crispy. Remove from the skillet and reserve.

Add the onion and garlic to the skillet and cook for 5 minutes, or until softened. Stir in the tomato sauce, chopped tomatoes, and basil, and season to taste with salt and pepper. Bring to a boil, lower the heat, and simmer the sauce for 5 minutes.

Meanwhile, bring a large pan of lightly salted water to a rapid boil. Add the macaroni and cook according to the package instructions, or until cooked but still firm.

Drain the macaroni thoroughly, return to the pan, and stir in the sauce, chicken, and mozzarella cheese. Spoon into a shallow ovenproof dish.

Sprinkle the pancetta over the macaroni. Sprinkle over the Gruyère and Parmesan cheeses. Place under the preheated broiler and cook for 5–10 minutes, or until golden-brown; turn the dish occasionally. Garnish and serve immediately.

Try this: FOR AN APPETIZER: 50   FOR DESSERT: 370

Chicken & Baby Vegetable Stir-Fry

SERVES 4

2 tbsp peanut oil
1 small red chile pepper,
   deseeded and finely
   chopped
5 oz chicken breast
   or thigh meat, skinned
   and cut into cubes
2 baby leeks, trimmed
   and sliced

12 asparagus spears, halved
1½ cups snow peas, trimmed
6–8 baby carrots, trimmed
   and halved lengthways
1 cup green beans, trimmed
   and diagonally sliced
16 baby sweet corn,
   diagonally halved
¼ cup chicken stock

2 tsp light soy sauce
1 tbsp dry sherry
1 tsp sesame oil
toasted sesame seeds,
   to garnish

Heat the wok until hot and add the oil. Add the chopped chile pepper and chicken and stir-fry for 4–5 minutes, or until the chicken is cooked and golden.

Increase the heat, add the leeks to the chicken, and stir-fry for 2 minutes. Add the asparagus spears, snow peas, baby carrots, green beans, and baby sweet corn. Stir-fry for 3–4 minutes, or until the vegetables soften slightly but still retain a slight crispness.

In a small bowl, mix together the chicken stock, soy sauce, dry sherry, and sesame oil. Pour into the wok, stir, and cook until heated through. Sprinkle with the toasted sesame seeds and serve immediately.

Try this: FOR AN APPETIZER: 58   FOR DESSERT: 380

Stir-fried Chicken with Basil

SERVES 4

3 tbsp sunflower oil
3 tbsp green curry paste
1 lb skinless, boneless
   chicken breast fillets,
   trimmed and cut
   into cubes
8 cherry tomatoes

½ cup coconut milk
2 tbsp soft brown sugar
2 tbsp Thai fish sauce
1 red chile pepper, deseeded
   and sliced
1 green chile pepper,
   deseeded and sliced

3 cups fresh torn
   basil leaves
sprigs of fresh cilantro,
   to garnish
freshly steamed white rice,
   to serve

Heat the wok, then add the oil and heat for 1 minute. Add the green curry paste and cook, stirring for 1 minute to release the flavor and cook the paste. Add the chicken and stir-fry over a high heat for 2 minutes, making sure the chicken is coated thoroughly with the green curry paste.

Reduce the heat under the wok, then add the cherry tomatoes and cook, stirring gently, for 2–3 minutes, or until the tomatoes burst and begin to disintegrate into the green curry paste.

Add half the coconut milk to the wok, along with the brown sugar, Thai fish sauce, and the red and green chile peppers. Stir-fry gently for 5 minutes, or until the sauce is amalgamated and the chicken is cooked thoroughly.

Just before serving, sprinkle the chicken with the torn basil leaves and add the remaining coconut milk, then serve immediately with freshly steamed white rice garnished with fresh cilantro sprigs.

Try this: FOR AN APPETIZER: 44   FOR DESSERT: 368

Chicken & Cashew Nuts

SERVES 4

1 lb skinless chicken,
   boneless breast fillets, cut
   into ½-inch cubes
1 medium egg white, beaten
1 tsp salt
1 tsp sesame oil
2 tsp cornstarch

1¼ cups peanut
   oil for deep-frying
2 tsp sunflower oil
⅓ cup unsalted cashews
4 green onions, shredded
¾ cup snow peas, diagonally
   sliced

1 tbsp Chinese rice wine
1 tbsp light soy sauce
shredded green onions,
   to garnish
freshly steamed white rice
   with fresh cilantro leaves,
   to serve

Place the cubes of chicken in a large bowl. Add the egg white, salt, sesame oil, and cornstarch. Mix well to ensure the chicken is coated thoroughly. Chill in the refrigerator for 20 minutes.

Heat the wok until hot and add the peanut oil; when hot, remove the wok from the heat and add the chicken. Stir continuously to prevent the chicken from sticking to the wok. When the chicken turns white, after about 2 minutes, remove it using a slotted spoon and reserve. Discard the oil.

Wipe the wok clean with a paper towel and heat the wok again until hot. Add the sunflower oil and heat. When hot, add the cashew nuts, green onions, and snow peas, and stir-fry for 1 minute.

Add the rice wine and soy sauce. Return the chicken to the wok and stir-fry for 2 minutes. Garnish with shredded green onions and serve immediately with freshly steamed rice sprinkled with fresh cilantro.

Try this: FOR AN APPETIZER: 48   FOR DESSERT: 360

Stir-fried Chicken with Spinach, Tomatoes & Pine Nuts

SERVES 4

½ cup pine nuts
2 tbsp sunflower oil
1 red onion, peeled and
 finely chopped
1 lb skinless, boneless
 chicken breast fillets,
 cut into strips

26 cherry tomatoes
 (about 1 lb), halved
8 cups baby spinach
 (about 8 oz), washed
salt and freshly ground
 black pepper
¼ tsp freshly

grated nutmeg
2 tbsp balsamic vinegar
⅓ cup raisins
freshly cooked egg noodles
 tossed in butter, to serve

Heat the wok and add the pine nuts. Dry-fry for about 2 minutes, shaking often to ensure that they toast but do not burn. Remove and reserve. Wipe any dust from the wok.

Heat the wok again and add the oil; when hot, add the red onion and stir-fry for 2 minutes. Add the chicken and stir-fry for 2–3 minutes, or until golden brown. Reduce the heat, toss in the cherry tomatoes, and stir-fry gently until the tomatoes start to disintegrate.

Add the baby spinach and stir-fry for 2–3 minutes, or until they start to wilt. Season to taste with salt and pepper, then sprinkle in the grated nutmeg and drizzle in the balsamic vinegar. Finally, stir in the raisins and reserved toasted pine nuts. Serve immediately on a bed of buttered egg noodles.

Try this: FOR AN APPETIZER: 52   FOR DESSERT: 354

Chicken with Noodles

SERVES 2–3

8 oz medium egg noodles
4 oz skinless, boneless
   chicken breast fillets
1 tbsp light soy sauce
2 tsp Chinese rice wine
   or dry sherry

5 tsp peanut oil
2 garlic cloves, peeled and
   finely chopped
¾ cup snow peas
1 oz smoked Canadian
   bacon,

   cut into fine strips
½ tsp sugar
2 green onions, peeled and
   finely chopped
1 tsp sesame oil

Cook the noodles according to the package directions. Drain and refresh under cold water. Drain again and reserve.

Slice the chicken into fine shreds and mix with 2 teaspoons of the light soy sauce and Chinese rice wine. Let marinate in the refrigerator for 10 minutes.

Heat a wok and add 2 teaspoons of the oil; when hot, stir-fry the chicken shreds for about 2 minutes, then transfer to a plate. Wipe the wok clean with a paper towel.

Return the wok to the heat and add the remaining oil. Add the garlic, then after 10 seconds add the snow peas and bacon. Stir-fry for a further 1 minute, then add the drained noodles, remaining soy sauce, sugar, and green onions. Stir-fry for a further 2 minutes then add the reserved chicken.

Stir-fry for a further 3–4 minutes until the chicken is cooked through. Add the sesame oil and mix together. Serve either hot or cold.

Try this: FOR AN APPETIZER: 36 FOR DESSERT: 372

Chicken Under a Brick

SERVES 4–6

4 lb chicken
¼ cup olive oil
sea salt and freshly
   ground black pepper

To garnish:
sprigs of fresh basil chives
tossed bitter lettuce leaves,
   to serve

Rinse the chicken and dry well, inside and out. Using poultry shears or kitchen scissors, cut along each side of the backbone of the chicken and discard or use for stock. Place the chicken, skin-side up, on a work surface and, using the palm of your hand, press down firmly to break the breast bone and flatten the bird.

Turn the chicken, breast-side up, and use a sharp knife to slit the skin between the breast and thigh on each side. Fold the legs in and push the drumstick bones through the slits. Tuck the wing under – the chicken should be as flat as possible.

Heat the olive oil in a large, heavy-based skillet until hot, but not smoking. Place the chicken in the pan, skin-side down, and place a flat lid or plate directly on top of the chicken. Top with a brick (hence the name) or 5 lb weight. Cook for 12–15 minutes, or until golden brown. Remove the weights and lid and, using a pair of tongs, turn the chicken carefully, then season to taste with salt and pepper. Cover and weigh down the lid again, then cook for 12–15 minutes longer, until the chicken is tender and the juices run clear when a thigh is pierced with a sharp knife or skewer.

Transfer the chicken to a serving plate and cover loosely with foil to keep warm. Let rest for at least 10 minutes before carving. Garnish with sprigs of basil and chives and serve with lettuce leaves.

Try this: FOR AN APPETIZER: 42   FOR DESSERT: 356

Mixed Vegetable & Chicken Pasta

SERVES 4

3 boneless and skinless
   chicken breasts
2 leeks
1 red onion
12 oz pasta shells
2 tbsp butter
2 tbsp olive oil

1 garlic clove,
   peeled and chopped
10 cherry tomatoes, halved
1 cup heavy cream
15-oz can asparagus
   tips, drained
salt and freshly ground

black pepper
1 cup sharp Cheddar cheese
   with chives, crumbled
green salad,
   to serve

Preheat the broiler just before using. Cut the chicken into thin strips. Trim the leeks, leaving some of the dark green tops, then shred and wash thoroughly in plenty of cold water. Peel the onion and cut into thin wedges.

Bring a large pan of lightly salted water to a rapid boil. Add the pasta and cook according to the package instructions, or until cooked but still firm.

Meanwhile, melt butter with the olive oil in a large heavy-based pan, add the chicken, and cook, stirring occasionally, for 8 minutes, or until browned all over. Add the leeks and onion and cook for 5 minutes, or until softened. Add the garlic and cherry tomatoes and cook for a further 2 minutes.

Stir the cream and asparagus tips into the chicken and vegetable mixture, bring to a boil slowly, then remove from the heat. Drain the pasta thoroughly and return to the pan. Pour the sauce over the pasta, season to taste with salt and pepper, then toss lightly.

Tip the pasta mixture into a gratin dish and sprinkle with the cheese. Cook under the preheated broiler for 5 minutes, or until bubbling and golden, turning the dish occasionally. Serve immediately with a green salad.

Try this: FOR AN APPETIZER: 64   FOR DESSERT: 350

Chicken Gorgonzola & Mushroom Macaroni

SERVES 4

1 lb macaroni
6 tbsp butter
3 cups button mushrooms, cleaned and sliced
3 cups baby button mushrooms, cleaned and halved
12 oz cooked chicken, skinned and chopped
2 tsp cornstarch
1¼ cups semi-skimmed milk
½ cup Gorgonzola cheese, chopped, plus extra to serve
2 tbsp freshly chopped sage
1 tbsp freshly chopped chives, plus extra chive leaves to garnish
salt and freshly ground black pepper

Bring a large pan of lightly salted water to a rapid boil. Add the macaroni and cook according to the package instructions, or until cooked but still firm.

Meanwhile, melt the butter in a large skillet, add the mushrooms, and cook for 5 minutes, or until golden, stirring occasionally. Add the chicken to the pan and cook for 4 minutes, or until heated through thoroughly and slightly golden, stirring occasionally.

Blend the cornstarch with a little of the milk in a measuring cup to form a smooth paste, then gradually blend in the remaining milk and pour into the skillet. Bring to a boil slowly, stirring constantly. Add the cheese and cook for 1 minute, stirring frequently until melted.

Stir the sage and chives into the skillet. Season to taste with salt and pepper, then heat through. Drain the macaroni thoroughly and return to the pan. Pour the chicken and mushroom sauce over the macaroni and toss lightly to coat. Tip into a warmed serving dish, and serve immediately with extra Gorgonzola cheese.

Try this: FOR AN APPETIZER: 62   FOR DESSERT: 378

Thai Chicken with Chili & Peanuts

SERVES 4

2 tbsp vegetable or
   peanut oil
1 garlic clove, peeled
   and finely chopped
1 tsp dried chile pepper
   flakes
12 oz boneless, skinless

chicken breast,
   finely sliced
1 tbsp Thai fish sauce
2 tbsp peanuts, roasted and
   roughly chopped
1½ cups sugar snap peas
3 tbsp chicken stock

1 tbsp light soy sauce
1 tbsp dark soy sauce
large pinch of sugar
freshly chopped cilantro,
   to garnish
boiled or steamed rice,
   to serve

Heat a wok or large skillet and add the oil; when hot, carefully swirl the oil around the wok until the sides are lightly coated with the oil. Add the garlic and stir-fry for 10–20 seconds, or until starting to brown. Add the chile pepper flakes and stir-fry for a few seconds more.

Add the finely sliced chicken to the wok and stir-fry for 2–3 minutes, or until the chicken has turned white.

Add the following ingredients, stirring well after each addition: fish sauce, peanuts, sugar snap peas, chicken stock, light and dark soy sauces, and sugar. Give a final stir.

Bring the contents of the wok to a boil, then simmer gently for 3–4 minutes, or until the chicken and vegetables are tender. Remove from the heat and tip into a warmed serving dish. Garnish with chopped cilantro and serve immediately with boiled or steamed rice.

Try this: FOR AN APPETIZER: 58   FOR DESSERT: 376

Pesto Chicken Tagliatelle

SERVES 4

2 tbsp olive oil
12 oz boneless and skinless
   chicken breasts, cut into
   chunks
6 tbsp butter
2 medium leeks, trimmed
   and sliced thinly

1¾ cups oyster mushrooms,
   trimmed and halved
3 cups small button
   mushrooms, cleaned
   and halved
1 lb fresh tagliatelle
4–6 tbsp pesto

1 cup crème fraîche or
   sour cream
1 cup freshly grated
   Parmesan cheese
salt and freshly ground
   black pepper

Heat the oil in a large skillet, add the chicken, and cook for 8 minutes, or until golden brown, stirring occasionally. Using a slotted spoon, remove the chicken from the pan, drain on a paper towel, and reserve.

Melt the butter in the skillet. Add the leeks and cook for 3–5 minutes, or until slightly softened, stirring occasionally. Add the oyster and button mushrooms, and cook for 5 minutes, or until browned, stirring occasionally.

Bring a large pan of lightly salted water to a rapid boil, add the tagliatelle, return to a boil, and cook for 4 minutes, or until cooked but still firm.

Add the chicken, pesto, and crème fraîche to the mushroom mixture. Stir, then heat through thoroughly. Stir in the grated Parmesan cheese and season to taste with salt and pepper.

Drain the tagliatelle thoroughly and pile onto warmed plates. Spoon over the sauce and serve immediately.

Try this: FOR AN APPETIZER: 46   FOR DESSERT: 354

Braised Chicken with Eggplant

SERVES 4

3 tbsp vegetable oil
12 chicken thighs
2 large eggplants,
  trimmed and cubed
4 garlic cloves, peeled
  and crushed
2 tsp freshly grated ginger
3¾ cups vegetable stock

2 tbsp light soy sauce
2 tbsp Chinese preserved
  black beans
6 green onions, trimmed
  and thinly sliced
  diagonally
1 tbsp cornstarch
1 tbsp sesame oil

green onion curls,
  to garnish
freshly cooked noodles
  or rice, to serve

Heat a wok or large skill and add the oil; when hot, add the chicken thighs and cook over a medium high heat for 5 minutes, or until browned all over. Transfer to a large plate and keep warm.

Add the eggplants to the wok and cook over a high heat for 5 minutes or until browned, turning occasionally. Add the garlic and ginger and stir-fry for 1 minute.

Return the chicken to the wok, pour in the stock, and add the soy sauce and black beans. Bring to a boil, then simmer for 20 minutes, or until the chicken is tender. Add the green onions after 10 minutes.

Blend the cornstarch with 2 tablespoons of water. Stir into the wok and simmer until the sauce has thickened. Stir in the sesame oil, heat for 30 seconds, then remove from the heat. Garnish with green onion tassels (see page 48) and serve immediately with noodles or rice.

Noodles with Turkey & Mushrooms

SERVES 4

8 oz dried egg noodles
1 tbsp peanut oil
1 red onion, peeled
  and sliced
2 tbsp freshly grated ginger
3 garlic cloves, peeled and
  finely chopped

12 oz turkey breast, skinned
  and cut into strips
2 cups button mushrooms
1¾ cups baby button
  mushrooms
2 tbsp dark soy sauce
2 tbsp hoisin sauce

2 tbsp dry sherry
4 tbsp vegetable stock
2 tsp cornstarch

Bring a large saucepan of lightly salted water to a boil and add the noodles. Cook for 3–5 minutes, then drain and plunge immediately into cold water. When cool, drain again and reserve.

Heat the wok and add the oil; when hot, add the onion and stir-fry for 3 minutes, until it starts to soften. Add the ginger and garlic and stir-fry for a further 3 minutes, then add the turkey strips and stir-fry for 4–5 minutes, until sealed and golden.

Clean and slice the button mushrooms into similar-sized pieces and add to the wok with the whole baby mushrooms. Stir-fry for 3–4 minutes, or until tender. When all the vegetables are tender and the turkey is cooked, add the soy sauce, hoisin sauce, sherry, and vegetable stock.

Mix the cornstarch with 2 tablespoons of water and add to the wok, then cook, stirring, until the sauce thickens. Add the drained noodles to the wok, then toss the mixture together and serve immediately.

Try this: FOR AN APPETIZER: 30 FOR DESSERT: 352

Turkey Tetrazzini

SERVES 4

10 oz green and
  white tagliatelle
4 tbsp butter
4 slices streaky bacon,
  diced
1 onion, peeled and
  finely chopped
2½ cups button mushrooms,
  thinly sliced

6 tbsp all-purpose flour
2 cups chicken stock
⅔ cup heavy cream
2 tbsp sherry
1 lb cooked turkey meat, cut
  into bite-sized pieces
1 tbsp freshly
  chopped parsley
freshly grated nutmeg

salt and freshly ground
  black pepper
½ cup Parmesan cheese,
  grated

To garnish:
freshly chopped parsley
Parmesan cheese, grated

Preheat the oven to 350°F. Lightly oil a large ovenproof dish. Bring a large saucepan of lightly salted water to a rapid boil. Add the tagliatelle and cook for 7–9 minutes, or until cooked but still firm. Drain well and reserve.

In a heavy-based saucepan, heat the butter and add the bacon. Cook for 2–3 minutes, or until crisp and golden. Add the onion and mushrooms and cook for 3–4 minutes, or until the vegetables are tender.

Stir in the flour and cook for 2 minutes. Remove from the heat and slowly stir in the stock. Return to the heat and cook, stirring until a smooth, thick sauce has formed. Add the tagliatelle, then pour in the cream and sherry. Add the turkey and parsley. Season to taste with the nutmeg and salt and pepper. Toss well to coat.

Turn the mixture into the prepared dish, spreading evenly. Sprinkle the top with the Parmesan cheese and bake in the preheated oven for 30–35 minutes, or until crisp, golden, and bubbling. Garnish with chopped parsley and Parmesan cheese. Serve straight from the dish.

Try this: FOR AN APPETIZER: 20   FOR DESSERT: 366

Creamy Turkey & Tomato Pasta

SERVES 4

4 tbsp olive oil
1 lb turkey breasts, cut into
   bite-sized pieces
32 cherry tomatoes (about
   1¼ lb), on the vine

2 garlic cloves, peeled
   and chopped
4 tbsp balsamic vinegar
4 tbsp freshly chopped basil
salt and black pepper

1 cup crème fraîche or
   sour cream
12 oz tagliatelle
shaved Parmesan cheese,
   to garnish

Preheat the oven to 400°F. Heat 2 tablespoons of the olive oil in a large skillet. Add the turkey and cook for 5 minutes, or until sealed, turning occasionally. Transfer to a roasting pan and add the remaining olive oil, the vine tomatoes, garlic, and balsamic vinegar. Stir well and season to taste with salt and pepper. Cook in the preheated oven for 30 minutes, or until the turkey is tender, turning the tomatoes and turkey once.

Meanwhile, bring a large pan of lightly salted water to a rapid boil. Add the pasta and cook according to the package instructions, or until cooked but still firm. Drain, return to the pan, and keep warm. Stir the basil and seasoning into the crème fraîche.

Remove the roasting pan from the oven and discard the vines. Stir the crème fraîche and basil mixture into the turkey and tomato mixture, and return to the oven for 1–2 minutes, or until thoroughly heated through.

Stir the turkey and tomato mixture into the pasta and toss lightly together. Tip into a warmed serving dish. Garnish with Parmesan cheese shavings and serve immediately.

Try this: FOR AN APPETIZER: 54   FOR DESSERT: 350

Turkey & Oven–roasted Vegetable Salad

SERVES 4

6 tbsp olive oil
3 medium zucchini, trimmed
   and sliced
2 yellow bell peppers,
   deseeded and sliced
1 cup pine nuts
10 oz macaroni

12 oz cooked turkey
10-oz jar or can chargrilled
   artichokes, drained
   and sliced
4 baby plum tomatoes,
   quartered
4 tbsp freshly

   chopped cilantro
1 garlic clove, peeled
   and chopped
3 tbsp balsamic vinegar
salt and freshly ground
   black pepper

Preheat the oven to 400˚F, 15 minutes before cooking. Line a large roasting pan with foil, pour in half the olive oil, and place in the oven for 3 minutes, or until hot. Remove from the oven, add the zucchini and bell peppers, and stir until evenly coated. Bake for 30–35 minutes, or until slightly charred, turning occasionally.

Add the pine nuts to the pan. Return to the oven and bake for 10 minutes, or until the pine nuts are toasted. Remove from the oven and let the vegetables cool completely.

Bring a large pan of lightly salted water to a rapid boil. Add the macaroni and cook according to the package instructions, or until cooked but still firm. Drain and refresh under cold running water, then drain thoroughly and place in a large salad bowl.

Cut the turkey into bite-sized pieces and add to the macaroni. Add the artichokes and tomatoes with the cooled vegetables and pan juices to the pan. Blend together the cilantro, garlic, remaining oil, vinegar, and seasoning. Pour over the salad, toss lightly and serve.

Try this: FOR AN APPETIZER: 38 FOR DESSERT: 372

Turkey with Oriental Mushrooms

SERVES 4

½ cup dried Chinese
  mushrooms
1 lb turkey breast steaks
⅔ cup turkey or chicken stock
2 tbsp peanut oil
1 red bell pepper, deseeded
  and sliced
3 cups sugar snap peas,

trimmed
1¾ cups shiitake
  mushrooms, cleaned
  and halved
1¾ cups oyster mushrooms,
  cleaned and halved
2 tbsp yellow bean sauce
2 tbsp soy sauce

1 tbsp hot chile sauce
freshly cooked noodles,
  to serve

Place the dried mushrooms in a small bowl, cover with almost boiling water, and let stand for 20–30 minutes. Drain and discard any woody stems from the mushrooms. Cut the turkey into thin strips.

Pour the turkey or chicken stock into a wok or large skillet and bring to a boil. Add the turkey and cook gently for 3 minutes, or until the turkey is sealed completely, then using a slotted spoon, remove from the wok and reserve. Discard any stock.

Wipe the wok clean and reheat, then add the oil. When the oil is almost smoking, add the drained turkey and stir-fry for 2 minutes.

Add the drained mushrooms to the wok with the red bell pepper, the sugar snap peas, and the shiitake and oyster mushrooms. Stir-fry for 2 minutes, then add the yellow bean sauce, soy sauce, and hot chili sauce.

Stir-fry the mixture for 1–2 minutes more, or until the turkey is cooked thoroughly and the vegetables are cooked but still retain a bite. Turn into a warmed serving dish and serve immediately with freshly cooked noodles.

Try this: FOR AN APPETIZER: 48   FOR DESSERT: 374

Spaghetti with Turkey & Bacon Sauce

SERVES 4

1 lb spaghetti
2 tbsp butter
8 oz smoked streaky bacon, rind removed
12 oz fresh turkey strips
1 onion, peeled

and chopped
1 garlic clove, peeled and chopped
3 medium eggs, beaten
1¼ cups heavy cream
salt and freshly ground

black pepper
1 cup freshly grated Parmesan cheese
2–3 tbsp freshly chopped cilantro, to garnish

Bring a large pan of lightly salted water to a rapid boil. Add the spaghetti and cook according to the package instructions, or until cooked but still firm.

Meanwhile, melt the butter in a large skillet. Using a sharp knife, cut the streaky bacon into small dice. Add the bacon to the pan with the turkey strips, and cook for 8 minutes, or until browned, stirring occasionally to prevent sticking. Add the onion and garlic, and cook for 5 minutes, or until softened, stirring occasionally.

Place the eggs and cream in a bowl and season to taste with salt and pepper. Beat together then pour into the skillet and cook, stirring, for 2 minutes, or until the mixture begins to thicken but does not scramble.

Drain the spaghetti thoroughly and return to the skillet. Pour over the sauce, add the grated Parmesan cheese, and toss lightly. Heat through for 2 minutes, or until piping hot. Tip into a warmed serving dish and sprinkle with freshly chopped cilantro. Serve immediately.

Try this: FOR AN APPETIZER: 40   FOR DESSERT: 360

Vegetarian

Pad Thai Noodles with Mushrooms

SERVES 4

4 oz flat rice noodles
or rice vermicelli
1 tbsp vegetable oil
2 garlic cloves, peeled
and finely chopped
1 medium egg,
lightly beaten
3 cups mixed mushrooms,

including shiitake, oyster,
field, button, and wild
mushrooms
2 tbsp lemon juice
1½ tbsp Thai fish sauce
½ tsp sugar
½ tsp cayenne pepper
2 green onions, trimmed

and cut into 1-inch pieces
½ cup fresh bean sprouts

To garnish:
chopped roasted peanuts
freshly chopped cilantro

Cook the noodles according to the package instructions. Drain well and reserve.

Heat a wok or large skillet. Add the oil and garlic. Fry until just golden. Add the egg and stir quickly to break it up.

Cook for a few seconds before adding the noodles and mushrooms. Scrape down the sides of the pan to ensure they mix with the egg and garlic.

Add the lemon juice, fish sauce, sugar, cayenne pepper, green onions, and half of the bean sprouts, stirring quickly all the time.

Cook over a high heat for a further 2–3 minutes, until everything is heated through.

Turn onto a serving plate. Top with the remaining bean sprouts. Garnish with the chopped peanuts and cilantro and serve immediately.

Try this: FOR AN APPETIZER: 36 FOR DESSERT: 380

Pearl Onion Risotto

SERVES 4

For the pearl onions:
1 tbsp olive oil
1 lb pearl onions, peeled
   and halved if large
pinch of sugar
1 tbsp freshly
   chopped thyme

For the risotto:
1 tbsp olive oil
1 small onion, peeled
   and finely chopped
2 garlic cloves, peeled
   and finely chopped
1¾ cups risotto rice
⅔ cup red wine

4¼ cups hot vegetable stock
½ cup low-fat soft
   goat's cheese
salt and freshly ground
   black pepper
sprigs of fresh thyme,
   to garnish

For the pearl onions, heat the olive oil in a saucepan and add the pearl onions with the sugar. Cover and cook over a low heat, stirring occasionally, for 20–25 minutes until caramelized. Uncover during the last 10 minutes of cooking.

Meanwhile, for the risotto, heat the oil in a large skillet and add the onion. Cook over a medium heat for 5 minutes, until softened. Add the garlic and cook for a further 30 seconds.

Add the risotto rice and stir well. Add the red wine and stir constantly, until the wine is almost completely absorbed by the rice. Begin adding the stock one ladleful at a time, stirring well and waiting until the last ladleful has been absorbed before stirring in the next. It will take 20–25 minutes to add all the stock, by which time the rice should be just cooked but still firm. Remove from the heat.

Add the thyme to the onions and cook briefly. Increase the heat and let the onion mixture bubble for 2–3 minutes, until almost evaporated. Add the onion mixture to the risotto, along with the goat's cheese. Stir well and season to taste with salt and pepper. Garnish with sprigs of fresh thyme and serve immediately.

Try this: FOR AN APPETIZER: 54   FOR DESSERT: 350

Hot & Spicy Red Cabbage with Apples

SERVES 8

7–9 cups red cabbage (about 2 lb), cored and shredded
2 large onions (about 1 lb), peeled and finely sliced
3–4 medium cooking apples (about 1 lb), peeled, cored and finely sliced
½ tsp mixed spice
1 tsp ground cinnamon
2 tbsp light brown sugar
salt and freshly ground black pepper
grated rind of 1 large orange
1 tbsp fresh orange juice
¼ cup apple juice
2 tbsp wine vinegar

To serve:
crème fraîche or sour cream
freshly ground black pepper

Preheat the oven to 300˚F. Put just enough cabbage in a large casserole dish to cover the bottom evenly. Place a layer of the onions and apples on top of the cabbage.

Sprinkle a little of the mixed spice, cinnamon, and sugar over the top. Season with salt and pepper.

Spoon over a small portion of the orange rind, orange juice, and apple juice.

Continue to layer the casserole dish with the ingredients in the same order until used up.

Pour the vinegar as evenly as possible over the top layer of the ingredients.

Cover the casserole dish with a close-fitting lid and bake in the preheated oven, stirring occasionally, for 2 hours until the cabbage is moist and tender. Serve immediately with the crème fraîche and black pepper.

Try this: FOR AN APPETIZER: 58 FOR DESSERT: 372

Carrot, Celeriac & Sesame Seed Salad

SERVES 6

1½ cups celeriac (about 8 oz)
2–3 medium carrots (about
    8 oz), peeled
⅓ cup seedless raisins
2 tbsp sesame seeds
freshly chopped parsley,

to garnish

For the lemon &
    chill dressing:
grated rind of 1 lemon
4 tbsp lemon juice

2 tbsp sunflower oil
2 tbsp clear honey
1 red bird's eye chile pepper,
    deseeded and chopped
salt and freshly ground
    black pepper

Slice the celeriac into thin matchsticks. Place in a small saucepan of boiling salted water and boil for 2 minutes.

Drain and rinse the celeriac in cold water and place in a mixing bowl.

Finely grate the carrot. Add the carrot and the raisins to the celeriac in the bowl.

Place the sesame seeds under a hot broiler or dry-fry in a skillet for 1–2 minutes, until golden brown, then let cool.

Make the dressing by whisking together the lemon rind, lemon juice, oil, honey, chile pepper, and seasoning, or by shaking thoroughly in a screw-topped jar.

Pour 2 tablespoons of the dressing over the salad and toss well. Turn into a serving dish and sprinkle over the toasted sesame seeds and chopped parsley. Serve the remaining dressing separately.

Try this: FOR AN APPETIZER: 64 FOR DESSERT: 362

Vegetarian Cassoulet

SERVES 4

1 cup dried navy beans,
   soaked overnight
2 medium onions
1 bay leaf
6 cups cold water
3 medium potatoes (about
   1¼ lb), peeled and cut
   into ½-inch slices
salt and freshly ground

black pepper
5 tsp olive oil
1 large garlic clove,
   peeled and crushed
2 leeks, trimmed and sliced
7-oz can chopped tomatoes
1 tsp dark brown sugar
1 tbsp freshly chopped thyme
2 tbsp freshly chopped

parsley
3 zucchini, trimmed
   and sliced

For the topping:
1 cup fresh white bread
   crumbs
¼ cup Cheddar cheese,
   finely grated

Preheat the oven to 350°F, 10 minutes before required. Drain the beans, rinse under cold running water, and put in a saucepan. Peel one of the onions and add to the beans with the bay leaf. Pour in the water. Bring to a rapid boil and cook for 10 minutes, then turn down the heat, cover, and simmer for 50 minutes, or until the beans are almost tender. Drain the beans, reserving the liquor but discarding the onion and bay leaf.

Cook the potatoes in a saucepan of lightly salted boiling water for 6–7 minutes, until almost tender when tested with the point of a knife. Drain and reserve.

Peel and chop the remaining onion. Heat the oil in a skillet and cook the onion with the garlic and leeks for 10 minutes, until softened. Stir in the tomatoes, sugar, thyme, and parsley. Stir in the beans, with 1¼ cups of the reserved liquor and season to taste. Simmer, uncovered, for 5 minutes. Layer the potato slices, zucchini, and ladlefuls of the bean mixture in a large flameproof casserole dish. To make the topping, mix together the bread crumbs and cheese and sprinkle over the top.

Bake in the preheated oven for 40 minutes, or until the vegetables are cooked through and the topping is golden brown and crisp. Serve immediately.

Layered Cheese & Herb Potato Cake

SERVES 4

6 medium waxy potatoes (about 2 lb)
3 tbsp freshly snipped chives
2 tbsp freshly chopped parsley
2 cups Cheddar cheese

2 large egg yolks
1 tsp paprika
2 cups fresh white bread crumbs
⅓ cup almonds, toasted and roughly chopped

4 tbsp butter, melted
salt and freshly ground black pepper
mixed salad or steamed vegetables, to serve

Preheat the oven to 350°F. Lightly oil and line the bottom of an 8-inch round cake pan with lightly oiled greaseproof or baking parchment paper. Peel and thinly slice the potatoes and reserve. Stir the chives, parsley, cheese, and egg yolks together in a small bowl and reserve. Mix the paprika into the bread crumbs.

Sprinkle the almonds over the bottom of the lined pan. Cover with half the potatoes, arranging them in layers, then sprinkle with the paprika-bread crumb mixture and season to taste with salt and pepper.

Spoon the cheese and herb mixture over the bread crumbs with a little more seasoning, then arrange the remaining potatoes on top. Drizzle over the melted butter and press the surface down firmly.

Bake in the preheated oven for 1¼ hours, or until golden and cooked through. Let the pan stand for 10 minutes before carefully turning out and serving in thick wedges. Serve immediately with salad or freshly cooked vegetables.

Try this: FOR AN APPETIZER: 58   FOR DESSERT: 368

Pasta with Raw Fennel, Tomato & Red Onions

SERVES 6

1 fennel bulb
6 medium tomatoes
   (about 1½ lb)
1 garlic clove
¼ small red onion

small handful fresh basil
small handful fresh mint
½ cup extra virgin olive oil,
   plus extra to serve
juice of 1 lemon

salt and freshly ground
   black pepper
1 lb penne or pennette
freshly grated Parmesan
   cheese, to serve

Trim the fennel and slice thinly. Stack the slices and cut into sticks, then cut crosswise again into fine dice. Deseed the tomatoes and chop them finely. Peel and finely chop or crush the garlic. Peel and finely chop or grate the onion.

Stack the basil leaves then roll up tightly. Slice crosswise into fine shreds. Finely chop the mint.

Place the chopped vegetables and herbs in a medium bowl. Add the olive oil and lemon juice and mix together. Season well with salt and pepper then let stand for 30 minutes to allow the flavors to develop.

Bring a large pan of salted water to a rapid boil. Add the pasta and cook according to the package instructions, or until cooked but still firm.

Drain the cooked pasta thoroughly. Transfer to a warmed serving dish, pour over the vegetable mixture, and toss. Serve with the grated Parmesan cheese and extra olive oil to drizzle over.

Try this: FOR AN APPETIZER: 50 FOR DESSERT: 380

Pasta with Walnut Sauce

SERVES 4

⅓ cup walnuts, toasted
3 green onions, trimmed
   and chopped
2 garlic cloves, peeled
   and sliced

1 tbsp freshly chopped
   parsley or basil
5 tbsp extra virgin olive oil
salt and freshly ground
   black pepper

2 cups broccoli florets
12 oz pasta shapes
1 red chile pepper, deseeded
   and finely chopped

Place the toasted walnuts in a blender or food processor with the chopped green onions, one of the garlic cloves, and the parsley or basil. Blend to a fairly smooth paste, then gradually add 3 tablespoons of the olive oil, until it is well mixed into the paste. Season the walnut paste to taste with salt and pepper and reserve.

Bring a large pan of lightly salted water to a rapid boil. Add the broccoli, return to a boil, and cook for 2 minutes. Remove the broccoli, using a slotted draining spoon, and refresh under cold running water. Drain again and pat dry on a paper towel.

Bring the water back to a rapid boil. Add the pasta and cook according to the package instructions, or until cooked but still firm.

Meanwhile, heat the remaining oil in a skillet. Add the remaining garlic and chile pepper. Cook gently for 2 minutes, or until softened. Add the broccoli and walnut paste. Cook for a further 3–4 minutes, or until heated through.

Drain the pasta thoroughly and transfer to a large warmed serving bowl. Pour over the walnut and broccoli sauce. Toss together, adjust the seasoning, and serve immediately.

Try this: FOR AN APPETIZER: 32   FOR DESSERT: 356

Melanzane Parmigiana

SERVES 4

2–3 eggplants (about 2 lb)
salt and freshly ground
   black pepper
5 tbsp olive oil
1 red onion, peeled
   and chopped
½ tsp mild paprika

⅔ cup dry red wine
⅔ cup vegetable stock
14-oz can chopped tomatoes
1 tsp tomato paste
1 tbsp freshly
   chopped oregano
1½ cups mozzarella cheese,

   thinly sliced
⅔ cup Parmesan cheese,
   coarsely grated
sprig of fresh basil,
   to garnish

Preheat the oven to 400°F, 15 minutes before cooking. Cut the eggplant lengthways into thin slices. Sprinkle with salt and let drain in a colander over a bowl for 30 minutes.

Meanwhile, heat 1 tablespoon of the olive oil in a saucepan and fry the onion for 10 minutes, until softened. Add the paprika and cook for 1 minute. Stir in the wine, stock, tomatoes, and tomato paste. Simmer, uncovered, for 25 minutes, or until fairly thick. Stir in the oregano and season to taste with salt and pepper. Remove from the heat.

Rinse the eggplant slices thoroughly under cold water and pat dry on a paper towel. Heat 2 tablespoons of the oil in a griddle pan and cook the eggplant in batches, for 3 minutes on each side, until golden. Drain well on a paper towel.

Pour half of the tomato sauce into the base of a large ovenproof dish. Cover with half the eggplant slices, then top with the mozzarella. Cover with the remaining eggplant slices and pour over the remaining tomato sauce. Sprinkle with the grated Parmesan cheese.

Bake in the preheated oven for 30 minutes, or until the eggplant slices are tender and the sauce is bubbling. Garnish with a sprig of fresh basil and let cool for a few minutes before serving.

Try this: FOR AN APPETIZER: 58 FOR DESSERT: 366

Rigatoni with Oven–dried Cherry Tomatoes & Mascarpone

SERVES 4

20 red cherry tomatoes
  (about 12 oz)
1 tsp superfine sugar
salt and freshly ground
  black pepper

2 tbsp olive oil
14 oz dried rigatoni
1 cup little green peas
2 tbsp mascarpone cheese
1 tbsp freshly chopped mint

1 tbsp freshly
  chopped parsley
sprigs of fresh mint,
  to garnish

Preheat the oven to 275°F. Halve the cherry tomatoes and place close together on a nonstick baking sheet, cut-side up. Sprinkle lightly with the sugar, then with a little salt and pepper. Bake in the preheated oven for 1¼ hours, or until dry, but not beginning to color. Let cool on the baking sheet. Put in a bowl, drizzle over the olive oil, and toss to coat.

Bring a large saucepan of lightly salted water to a rapid boil and cook the pasta for about 10 minutes or until cooked but still firm. Add the petits pois 2–3 minutes before the end of the cooking time. Drain thoroughly and return the pasta and the petits pois to the saucepan.

Add the mascarpone to the saucepan. When melted, add the tomatoes, mint, parsley, and a little black pepper. Toss gently together, then transfer to a warmed serving dish or individual plates and garnish with sprigs of fresh mint. Serve immediately.

Try this: FOR AN APPETIZER: 54   FOR DESSERT: 350

Spaghetti with Pesto

SERVES 4

3½ cups freshly grated
  Parmesan cheese,
  plus extra to serve
1 cup fresh basil leaves,
  plus extra to garnish

6 tbsp pine nuts
3 large garlic cloves,
  peeled
1 cup extra virgin olive oil,
  plus more if necessary

salt and freshly
  ground pepper
14 oz spaghetti

To make the pesto, place the Parmesan cheese in a food processor with the basil leaves, pine nuts, and garlic, and process until well blended.

With the motor running, gradually pour in the extra virgin olive oil, until a thick sauce forms. Add a little more oil if the sauce seems too thick. Season to taste with salt and pepper. Transfer to a bowl, cover, and store in the refrigerator until required.

Bring a large pan of lightly salted water to a rapid boil. Add the spaghetti and cook according to the package instructions, or until cooked but still firm

Drain the spaghetti thoroughly and return to the pan. Stir in the pesto and toss lightly. Heat through gently, then tip the pasta into a warmed serving dish or spoon onto individual plates. Garnish with basil leaves and serve immediately with extra Parmesan cheese.

Try this: FOR AN APPETIZER: 36   FOR DESSERT: 376

Pasta Shells with Broccoli & Capers

SERVES 4

14 oz conchiglie (shells)
2 cups broccoli florets, cut into small pieces
5 tbsp olive oil
1 large onion, peeled and finely chopped
4 tbsp capers in brine, rinsed and drained
½ tsp dried chile pepper flakes (optional)
1½ cups freshly grated Parmesan cheese, plus extra to serve
½ cup pecorino or Parmesan cheese, grated
salt and freshly ground black pepper
2 tbsp freshly chopped flat-leaf parsley, to garnish

Bring a large pan of lightly salted water to a rapid boil. Add the conchiglie, return to a boil, and cook for 6 minutes. Add the broccoli to the pan. Return to a boil and continue cooking for 4–6 minutes, or until the conchiglie is cooked but still firm.

Meanwhile, heat the olive oil in a large skillet, add the onion, and cook for 5 minutes, or until softened, stirring frequently. Stir in the capers and chile flakes, if using, and cook for a further 2 minutes.

Drain the pasta and broccoli and add to the skillet. Toss the ingredients to mix thoroughly. Sprinkle over the cheeses, then stir until the cheeses have just melted. Season to taste with salt and pepper, then tip into a warmed serving dish. Garnish with chopped parsley and serve immediately with extra Parmesan cheese.

Try this: FOR AN APPETIZER: 52   FOR DESSERT: 358

Venetian Herb Orzo

SERVES 4-6

7 cups baby spinach leaves	6 green onions, trimmed	salt and freshly ground
5 cups arugula	3 tbsp extra virgin olive oil,	black pepper
2 cups flat-leaf parsley	plus more if required	
few leaves of fresh mint	11 oz orzo	

Rinse the spinach leaves in several changes of cold water and reserve. Finely chop the arugula with the parsley and mint. Thinly slice the green of the green onions.

Bring a large saucepan of water to a boil, add the spinach, arugula and herbs, and the green onions, and cook for about 10 seconds. Remove and rinse under cold running water. Drain well and, using your hands, squeeze out all the excess moisture.

Place the spinach, arugula and herbs, and the green onions in a food processor. Blend for 1 minute, then, with the motor running, gradually pour in the olive oil until the sauce is well blended.

Meanwhile, bring a large pan of lightly salted water to a rapid boil. Add the pasta and cook according to the package instructions, or until cooked but still firm. Drain thoroughly and place in a large warmed bowl.

Add the spinach sauce to the orzo and stir lightly until the orzo is well coated. Stir in an extra tablespoon of olive oil if the mixture seems too thick. Season well with salt and pepper. Serve immediately on warmed plates or let cool to room temperature.

Fusilli with Zucchini & Sun-dried Tomatoes

SERVES 6

5 tbsp olive oil
1 large onion, peeled
   and thinly sliced
2 garlic cloves, peeled
   and finely chopped
4–5 medum zucchini (about
   1½ lb), trimmed and sliced

14-oz can chopped
   plum tomatoes
12 sun-dried tomatoes,
   cut into thin strips
salt and freshly ground
   black pepper
1 lb fusilli

2 tbsp butter, diced
2 tbsp freshly chopped basil
   or flat-leaf parsley
grated Parmesan or
   pecorino cheese,
   for serving

Heat 2 tablespoons of the olive oil in a large skillet, add the onion, and cook for 5–7 minutes, or until softened. Add the chopped garlic and zucchini slices and cook for a further 5 minutes, stirring occasionally.

Stir the chopped tomatoes and the sun-dried tomatoes into the skillet and season to taste with salt and pepper. Cook until the zucchini is just tender and the sauce is slightly thickened.

Bring a large pan of lightly salted water to a rapid boil. Add the fusilli and cook according to the package instructions, or until cooked but still firm.

Drain the fusilli thoroughly and return to the pan. Add the butter and remaining oil and toss to coat. Stir the chopped basil or parsley into the zucchini mixture and pour over the fusilli. Toss and tip into a warmed serving dish. Serve with grated Parmesan or pecorino cheese.

Try this: FOR AN APPETIZER: 50   FOR DESSERT: 372

Four-cheese Tagliatelle

SERVES 4

1¼ cups heavy cream
4 garlic cloves, peeled
    and lightly crushed
¾ cup Fontina
    cheese, diced
¾ cup Gruyère
    cheese, grated

¾ cup mozzarella cheese,
    preferably, diced
1 cup Parmesan cheese,
    grated, plus extra
    to serve
salt and freshly ground
    black pepper

10 oz fresh green tagliatelle
1–2 tbsp freshly
    snipped chives
fresh basil leaves,
    to garnish

Place the heavy cream with the garlic cloves in a medium pan and heat gently until small bubbles begin to form around the edge of the pan. Using a slotted spoon, remove and discard the garlic cloves.

Add all the cheeses to the pan and stir until melted. Season with a little salt and a lot of black pepper. Keep the sauce warm over a low heat, but do not allow it to boil.

Meanwhile, bring a large pan of lightly salted water to a rapid boil. Add the taglietelle, return to a boil, and cook for 2–3 minutes, or until cooked but still firm.

Drain the pasta thoroughly and return to the pan. Pour the sauce over the pasta, add the chives, then toss lightly until well coated. Tip into a warmed serving dish or spoon onto individual plates. Garnish with a few basil leaves and serve immediately with extra Parmesan cheese.

Try this: FOR AN APPETIZER: 28   FOR DESSERT: 378

Zucchini Lasagne

SERVES 8

2 tbsp olive oil
1 medium onion, peeled
  and finely chopped
3 cups mushrooms, cleaned
  and thinly sliced
3–4 zucchini, trimmed
  and thinly sliced
2 garlic cloves, peeled

and finely chopped
½ tsp dried thyme
1–2 tbsp freshly chopped
  basil or flat-leaf parsley
salt and freshly ground
  black pepper
1 quantity prepared white
  sauce (see page 148)

12 oz lasagne
  sheets, cooked
2 cups mozzarella cheese,
  grated
1 cup Parmesan cheese,
  grated
14-oz can chopped
  tomatoes, drained

Preheat the oven to 400˚F, 15 minutes before cooking. Heat the oil in a large skillet, add the onion, and cook for 3–5 minutes. Add the mushrooms, cook for 2 minutes then add the zucchini and cook for a further 3–4 minutes, or until tender. Stir in the garlic, thyme, and basil or parsley, and season to taste with salt and pepper. Remove from the heat and reserve.

Spoon one-third of the white sauce onto the bottom of a lightly oiled large baking dish. Arrange a layer of lasagne over the sauce. Spread half the zucchini mixture over the pasta, then sprinkle with some of the mozzarella cheese and some of the Parmesan cheese. Repeat with more white sauce and another layer of lasagne, then cover with half the drained tomatoes.

Cover the tomatoes with lasagne, the remaining zucchini mixture, and some mozzarella cheese and Parmesan cheese. Repeat the layers ending with a layer of lasagne sheets, white sauce, and the remaining Parmesan cheese. Bake in the preheated oven for 35 minutes, or until golden. Serve immediately.

Try this: FOR AN APPETIZER: 48   FOR DESSERT: 374

Spicy Cucumber Stir-Fry

SERVES 4

¼ cup black beans, soaked in
   cold water, overnight
1½ cucumbers
2 tsp salt
1 tbsp peanut oil

½ tsp mild chili powder
4 garlic cloves, peeled
   and crushed
5 tbsp vegetable stock
1 tsp sesame oil

1 tbsp freshly
   chopped parsley,
   to garnish

Rinse the soaked beans thoroughly, then drain. Place in a saucepan, cover with cold water, and bring to the boil, skimming off any scum that rises to the surface. Boil for 10 minutes, then reduce the heat, and simmer for 1–1½ hours. Drain and reserve.

Peel the cucumbers, slice lengthways, and remove the seeds. Cut into 1-inch slices and place in a colander over a bowl. Sprinkle the salt over the cucumber and let stand for 30 minutes. Rinse thoroughly in cold water, drain, and pat dry with a paper towel.

Heat a wok or large skillet, add the oil, and when hot, add the chili powder, garlic, and black beans, and stir-fry for 30 seconds. Add the cucumber and stir-fry for 20 seconds.

Pour the stock into the wok and cook for 3–4 minutes, or until the cucumber is tender. The liquid will have evaporated at this stage. Remove from the heat and stir in the sesame oil. Turn into a warmed serving dish, garnish with chopped parsley, and serve immediately.

Try this: FOR AN APPETIZER: 64 FOR DESSERT: 356

Chinese Egg Fried Rice

SERVES 4

1½ cups long-grain rice
1 tbsp dark sesame oil
2 large eggs
1 tbsp sunflower oil
2 garlic cloves,
   peeled and crushed
1-inch piece fresh ginger,
   peeled and grated

1 carrot, peeled and
   cut into matchsticks
1½ cups snow peas, halved
8-oz can water chestnuts,
   drained and halved
1 yellow bell pepper,
   deseeded and diced
4 green onions, trimmed

   and finely shredded
2 tbsp light soy sauce
½ tsp paprika
salt and freshly ground
   black pepper

Bring a saucepan of lightly salted water to the boil, add the rice, and cook for 15 minutes or according to the package instructions. Drain and let cool.

Heat a wok or large skillet and add the sesame oil. Beat the eggs in a small bowl and pour into the hot wok. Using a fork, draw the egg in from the sides of the pan to the center until it sets, then turn over and cook the other side. When set and golden turn out onto a board. Let cool, then cut into thin strips.

Wipe the wok clean with a paper towel, return to the heat, and add the sunflower oil. When hot, add the garlic and ginger and stir-fry for 30 seconds. Add the remaining vegetables and continue to stir-fry for 3–4 minutes, or until tender but still crisp.

Stir the reserved cooked rice into the wok with the soy sauce and paprika and season to taste with salt and pepper. Fold in the cooked egg strips and heat through. Tip into a warmed serving dish and serve immediately.

Baked Macaroni Cheese

SERVES 8

1 lb macaroni
6 tbsp butter
1 onion, peeled and
   finely chopped
⅓ cup all-purpose flour
4¼ cups milk
1–2 dried bay leaves
½ tsp dried thyme

salt and freshly ground
   black pepper
cayenne pepper
freshly grated nutmeg
2 small leeks, trimmed,
   finely chopped, cooked
   and drained
1 tbsp Dijon mustard

3½ cups sharp
   Cheddar cheese, grated
2 tbsp dried bread crumbs
¼ cup freshly grated
   Parmesan cheese
basil sprig, to garnish

Preheat the oven to 375°F, 10 minutes before cooking. Bring a large pan of lightly salted water to a rapid boil. Add the macaroni and cook according to the package instructions, or until cooked but still firm. Drain thoroughly and reserve.

Meanwhile, melt 4 tablespoons of the butter in a large, heavy-based saucepan, add the onion, and cook, stirring frequently, for 5–7 minutes, or until softened. Sprinkle in the flour and cook, stirring constantly, for 2 minutes. Remove the pan from the heat, stir in the milk, return to the heat, and cook, stirring, until a smooth sauce has formed.

Add the bay leaf and thyme to the sauce and season to taste with salt, pepper, cayenne pepper, and freshly grated nutmeg. Simmer for about 15 minutes, stirring frequently, until thickened and smooth.

Remove the sauce from the heat. Add the cooked leeks, mustard, and Cheddar cheese, and stir until the cheese has melted. Stir in the macaroni then tip into a lightly oiled baking dish.

Sprinkle the bread crumbs and Parmesan cheese over the macaroni. Dot with the remaining butter, then bake in the preheated oven for 1 hour, or until golden. Garnish with a basil sprig and serve immediately.

Try this: FOR AN APPETIZER: 58   FOR DESSERT: 364

Coconut–baked Zucchini

SERVES 4

3 tbsp peanut oil
1 onion, peeled and
  finely sliced
4 garlic cloves, peeled
  and crushed

½ tsp chili powder
1 tsp ground coriander
6–8 tbsp shredded coconut
1 tbsp tomato paste
4 medium zucchini (about

1½ lb), thinly sliced
freshly chopped parsley,
  to garnish

Preheat the oven to 350°F, 10 minutes before cooking. Lightly oil a 1-quart ovenproof casserole dish. Heat a wok and add the oil; when hot, add the onion and stir-fry for 2–3 minutes, or until softened. Add the garlic, chili powder and coriander, and stir-fry for 1–2 minutes.

Pour 1¼ cups of cold water into the wok and bring to a boil. Add the coconut and tomato paste and simmer for 3–4 minutes; most of the water will evaporate at this stage. Spoon 4 tablespoons of the spice and coconut mixture into a small bowl and reserve.

Stir the zucchini into the remaining spice and coconut mixture, coating well. Spoon the zucchini into the oiled casserole dish and sprinkle the reserved spice and coconut mixture evenly over the top. Bake, uncovered, in the preheated oven for 15–20 minutes, or until golden. Garnish with chopped parsley and serve immediately.

Try this: FOR AN APPETIZER: 48   FOR DESSERT: 372

Mixed Vegetables Stir–Fry

SERVES 4

2 tbsp peanut oil
4 garlic cloves, peeled
   and finely sliced
1-inch piece fresh ginger,
   peeled and finely sliced
½ cup broccoli florets
¾ cup snow peas, trimmed
1 medium carrots, peeled

and cut into matchsticks
1 green bell pepper,
   deseeded and cut
   into strips
1 red bell pepper, deseeded
   and cut into strips
1 tbsp soy sauce
1 tbsp hoisin sauce

1 tsp sugar
salt and freshly ground
   black pepper
4 green onions, trimmed
   and shredded,
   to garnish

Heat a wok and add the oil; when hot, add the garlic and ginger slices and stir-fry for 1 minute.

Add the broccoli florets to the wok, stir-fry for 1 minute, then add the snow peas, carrots, and the bell peppers, and stir-fry for a further 3–4 minutes, or until tender but still crisp.

Blend the soy sauce, hoisin sauce, and sugar, in a small bowl. Stir well, season to taste with salt and pepper, and pour into the wok. Transfer the vegetables to a warmed serving dish. Garnish with shredded green onions and serve immediately.

Try this: FOR AN APPETIZER: 50 FOR DESSERT: 352

Rigatoni with Gorgonzola & Walnuts

SERVES 4

14 oz rigatoni
4 tbsp butter
1 cup Gorgonzola cheese, crumbled
2 tbsp brandy, optional
1 cup heavy cream

⅔ cup walnuts, lightly toasted and coarsely chopped
1 tbsp freshly chopped basil
1 cup freshly grated Parmesan cheese

salt and freshly ground black pepper

To serve:
cherry tomatoes
fresh green lettuce

Bring a large pan of lightly salted water to a rapid boil. Add the rigatoni and cook according to the package instructions, or until cooked but still firm. Drain the pasta thoroughly, reserve, and keep warm.

Melt the butter in a large saucepan or wok over a medium heat. Add the Gorgonzola cheese and stir until just melted. Add the brandy, if using, and cook for 30 seconds, then pour in the cream and cook for 1–2 minutes, stirring until the sauce is smooth.

Stir in the walnut pieces, basil, and half the Parmesan cheese, then add the rigatoni. Season to taste with salt and pepper. Return to the heat, stirring frequently, until heated through. Divide the pasta among 4 warmed pasta bowls, sprinkle with the remaining Parmesan cheese, and serve immediately with cherry tomatoes and fresh green lettuce.

Try this: FOR AN APPETIZER: 56   FOR DESSERT: 374

Basmati Rice with Saffron & Fava Beans

SERVES 4

1 medium egg
2 tbsp olive oil
1 tbsp freshly chopped
    mixed herbs
salt and freshly ground

black pepper
1 cup basmati rice
4 tbsp butter
1 small onion, peeled
    and finely chopped

1 garlic clove, peeled
    and finely chopped
large pinch saffron strands
1½ cups shelled fava beans,
    blanched

Beat the egg with 1 teaspoon of olive oil and the herbs. Season lightly with salt and pepper. Heat the remaining teaspoon of olive oil in a wok or small skillet. Pour half the egg mixture into the wok, tilting it to coat the bottom. Cook gently until set on top. Flip over and cook for a further 30 seconds. Transfer to a plate and repeat, using the remaining mixture, then reserve.

Wash the rice in several changes of water until the water remains relatively clear. Add the drained rice to a large saucepan of boiling salted water and cook for 12–15 minutes, until tender. Drain well and reserve.

Heat the butter with the remaining oil in a wok and add the onion and garlic. Cook gently for 3–4 minutes, until the onion is softened. Add the saffron and stir well. Add the drained rice and stir before adding the fava beans. Cook for a further 2–3 minutes, or until heated through.

Meanwhile, roll the egg pancakes into cigar shapes, then slice crosswise into strips. To serve, divide the rice between individual serving bowls and top with the egg strips.

Try this: FOR AN APPETIZER: 58   FOR DESSERT: 358

Chinese Cabbage with Sweet & Sour Sauce

SERVES 4

1 head Chinese cabbage	2 tbsp brown sugar	3 tbsp sunflower oil
1¼ cups pak choi	3 tbsp red wine vinegar	1 tbsp butter
1 tbsp cornstarch	3 tbsp orange juice	1 tsp salt
1 tbsp soy sauce	2 tbsp tomato paste	2 tbsp toasted sesame seeds

Discard any tough outer leaves and stalks from the Chinese cabbage and pak choi and wash well. Drain thoroughly and pat dry with a paper towel. Shred the Chinese cabbage and pak choi lengthways. Reserve.

In a small bowl, blend the cornstarch with 4 tablespoons of water. Add the soy sauce, sugar, vinegar, orange juice, and tomato paste and stir until blended thoroughly.

Pour the sauce into a small saucepan and bring to a boil. Simmer gently for 2–3 minutes, or until the sauce is thickened and smooth.

Meanwhile, heat a wok or large skillet and add the sunflower oil and butter. When melted, add the prepared Chinese cabbage and pak choi, sprinkle with the salt, and stir-fry for 2 minutes. Reduce the heat and cook gently for a further 1–2 minutes or until tender.

Transfer the Chinese cabbage and pak choi to a warmed serving platter and drizzle over the warm sauce. Sprinkle with the toasted sesame seeds and serve immediately.

Try this: FOR AN APPETIZER: 36   FOR DESSERT: 368

Eggplant & Tomato Layer

SERVES 4

2 eggplants (about 1½ lb),
    trimmed and thinly sliced
6 tbsp olive oil
1 onion, peeled and
    finely sliced
1 garlic clove, peeled
    and crushed
14-oz can chopped tomatoes

¼ cup red wine
½ tsp sugar
salt and freshly ground
    black pepper
4 tbsp butter
3 tbsp flour
2 cups milk
8 oz fresh egg lasagne

2 medium eggs, beaten
1 cup Greek yogurt
¾ cup mozzarella
    cheese, grated
fresh basil leaves,
    to garnish

Preheat the oven to 375°F, 10 minutes before cooking. Brush the eggplant slices with 5 tablespoons of the olive oil and place on a baking sheet. Bake in the preheated oven for 20 minutes, or until tender. Remove from the oven and increase the temperature to 400°F.

Heat the remaining oil in a heavy-based pan. Add the onion and garlic, cook for 2–3 minutes, then add the tomatoes, wine, and sugar. Season to taste with salt and pepper, then simmer for 20 minutes.

Melt the butter in another pan. Stir in the flour, cook for 2 minutes, then whisk in the milk. Cook for 2–3 minutes, or until thickened. Season to taste.

Pour a little white sauce into a lightly oiled, medium baking dish. Cover with a layer of lasagne, spread with tomato sauce, then add some of the eggplant. Cover thinly with white sauce and sprinkle with a little cheese. Continue to layer in this way, finishing with a layer of lasagne.

Beat together the eggs and yogurt. Season, then pour over the lasagne. Sprinkle with the remaining cheese and bake in the preheated oven for 25–30 minutes, or until golden. Garnish with basil leaves and serve.

    Try this: FOR AN APPETIZER: 54   FOR DESSERT: 350

Baked Macaroni with Mushrooms & Leeks

SERVES 4

2 tbsp olive oil
1 onion, peeled and
  finely chopped
1 garlic clove, peeled
  and crushed
2 small leeks, trimmed
  and chopped

6½ cups assorted wild
  mushrooms, trimmed
¼ cup white wine
6 tbsp butter
⅔ cup crème fraîche or
  heavy cream
salt and freshly ground

black pepper
12 oz short macaroni
1½ cups fresh white
  bread crumbs
1 tbsp freshly chopped
  parsley, to garnish

Preheat the oven to 425° F, 15 minutes before cooking. Heat 1 tablespoon of the olive oil in a large skillet, add the onion and garlic, and cook for 2 minutes. Add the leeks, mushrooms, and 2 tablespoons of the butter, then cook for 5 minutes. Pour in the white wine, cook for 2 minutes, then stir in the crème fraîche. Season to taste with salt and pepper.

Meanwhile, bring a large pan of lightly salted water to a rapid boil. Add the macaroni and cook according to the package instructions, or until cooked but still firm.

Melt 2 tablespoons of the butter with the remaining oil in a small skillet. Add the bread crumbs and fry until just beginning to turn golden-brown. Drain on a paper towel.

Drain the pasta thoroughly, toss in the remaining butter, then tip into a lightly oiled, shallow, medium baking dish. Cover the pasta with the leek and mushroom mixture, then sprinkle with the fried bread crumbs. Bake in the preheated oven for 5–10 minutes, or until golden and crisp. Garnish with chopped parsley and serve.

 Try this: FOR AN APPETIZER: 64   FOR DESSERT: 376

Bean & Cashew Stir-Fry

SERVES 4

3 tbsp sunflower oil
1 onion, peeled and
   finely chopped
1 celery stalk, trimmed
   and chopped
10-inch piece fresh ginger,
   peeled and grated
2 garlic cloves, peeled
   and crushed
1 red chile pepper, deseeded
and finely chopped
1½ cups fine green beans,
   trimmed and halved
2 cups snow peas, sliced
   diagonally into three
½ cup unsalted cashew nuts
1 tsp brown sugar
½ cup vegetable stock
2 tbsp dry sherry
1 tbsp light soy sauce
1 tsp red wine vinegar
salt and freshly ground
   black pepper
freshly chopped cilantro,
   to garnish

Heat a wok or large skillet and add the oil; when hot, add the onion and celery and stir-fry gently for 3–4 minutes, or until softened.

Add the ginger, garlic, and chile pepper to the wok and stir-fry for 30 seconds. Stir in the green beans, snow peas, and cashews, and continue to stir-fry for 1–2 minutes, or until the nuts are golden brown.

Dissolve the sugar in the stock, then blend with the sherry, soy sauce, and vinegar. Stir into the bean mixture and bring to a boil. Simmer gently, stirring occasionally for 3–4 minutes, or until the beans and snow peas are tender but still crisp and the sauce has thickened slightly. Season to taste with salt and pepper. Transfer to a warmed serving bowl or spoon onto individual plates. Sprinkle with freshly chopped cilantro and serve immediately.

Try this: FOR AN APPETIZER: 48   FOR DESSERT: 370

Rice with Squash & Sage

SERVES 4-6

1 lb butternut squash
6 tbsp unsalted butter
1 small onion, peeled
    and finely chopped
3 garlic cloves, peeled
    and crushed

2 tbsp freshly
    chopped sage
4¼ cups vegetable stock
2¼ cups arborio or
    risotto rice
½ cup pine nuts, toasted

½ cup freshly grated
    Parmesan cheese
freshly snipped chives,
    to garnish
salt and freshly ground
    black pepper

Peel the squash, cut in half lengthways, and remove seeds and stringy flesh. Cut the remaining flesh into small cubes and reserve.

Heat the wok, add the butter, and heat until foaming, then add the onion, garlic, and sage, and stir-fry for 1 minute.

Add the squash to the wok and stir-fry for a further 10–12 minutes, or until the squash is tender. Remove from the heat.

Meanwhile, bring the vegetable stock to a boil and add the rice. Cook for 8–10 minutes, or until the rice is just tender but still wet.

Add the cooked rice to the squash mixture. Stir in the pine nuts and Parmesan cheese, and season to taste with salt and pepper. Garnish with snipped chives and serve immediately.

Try this: FOR AN APPETIZER: 58   FOR DESSERT: 372

Thai-style Cauliflower & Potato Curry

SERVES 4

9–12 small new potatoes
    (about 1 lb), peeled and
    halved or quartered
1¼ cups cauliflower florets
3 garlic cloves,
    peeled and crushed
1 onion, peeled and
    finely chopped

½ cup ground almonds
1 tsp ground coriander
½ tsp ground cumin
½ tsp turmeric
3 tbsp peanut oil
salt and freshly ground
    black pepper
6 tbsp coconut milk

1 cup vegetable stock
1 tbsp mango chutney
sprigs of fresh cilantro,
    to garnish
freshly cooked long-grain
    rice, to serve

Bring a saucepan of lightly salted water to a boil, add the potatoes, and cook for 15 minutes, or until just tender. Drain and let cool. Boil the cauliflower for 2 minutes, then drain and refresh under cold running water. Drain again and reserve.

Meanwhile, blend the garlic, onion, ground almonds, and spices with 2 tablespoons of the oil, along with salt and pepper to taste, in a food processor until a smooth paste is formed. Heat a wok and add the remaining oil; when hot, add the spice paste and cook for 3–4 minutes, stirring continuously.

Add the coconut milk to the wok. Pour in the stock, cook for 2–3 minutes, then stir in the cooked potatoes and cauliflower.

Stir in the mango chutney and heat through for 3–4 minutes or until piping hot. Tip into a warmed serving dish, garnish with sprigs of fresh cilantro, and serve immediately with freshly cooked rice.

Try this: FOR AN APPETIZER: 30   FOR DESSERT: 378

Spiced Tomato Pilau

SERVES 2-3

1¼ cups basmati rice
3 tbsp unsalted butter
4 green cardamom pods
2 star anise
4 whole cloves
10 black peppercorns

2-inch piece cinnamon stick
1 large red onion, peeled
  and finely sliced
6-oz canned chopped
  tomatoes
salt and freshly ground

black pepper
sprigs of fresh cilantro,
  to garnish

Wash the rice in several changes of water until the water remains relatively clear. Drain the rice and cover with fresh water. Let soak for 30 minutes. Drain well and reserve.

Heat the wok, then melt the butter and add the cardamoms, star anise, cloves, black peppercorns, and the cinnamon stick. Cook gently for 30 seconds. Increase the heat and add the onion. Stir-fry for 7–8 minutes, until tender and starting to brown. Add the drained rice and cook a further 2–3 minutes.

Sieve the tomatoes and mix with sufficient warm water to make 2 cups. Pour this into the wok, season to taste with salt and pepper, and bring to a boil.

Cover, reduce the heat to low, and cook for 10 minutes. Remove the wok from the heat and let stand, covered, for a further 10 minutes. Do not lift the lid during cooking or resting. Finally, uncover and mix well with a fork, heat for 1 minute, then garnish with the sprigs of fresh cilantro and serve immediately.

Try this: FOR AN APPETIZER: 52   FOR DESSERT: 366

Dinner Parties & Entertaining

Creamy Salmon
with Dill in Phyllo Baskets

SERVES 4

1 bay leaf
6 black peppercorns
1 large sprig fresh parsley
6 oz salmon fillet
4 large sheets phyllo dough

oil cooking spray
4 cups baby spinach leaves
8 tbsp plain yogurt
2 tsp Dijon mustard
2 tbsp freshly chopped dill

salt and freshly ground
black pepper

Preheat the oven to 400˚F. Place the bay leaf, peppercorns, parsley, and salmon in a skillet and add enough water to barely cover the fish.

Bring to a boil, reduce the heat, and poach the fish for 5 minutes, until the fish flakes easily. Remove it from the pan. Reserve.

Spray each sheet of phyllo dough lightly with the oil. Scrunch up the dough to make a nest shape approximately 5 inches in diameter.

Place on a lightly oiled baking sheet and cook in the preheated oven for 10 minutes, until golden and crisp.

Blanch the spinach in a pan of lightly salted boiling water for 2 minutes. Drain thoroughly and keep warm.

Mix the yogurt, mustard, and dill together, then warm gently. Season to taste with salt and pepper. Divide the spinach between the phyllo nests and flake the salmon onto the spinach.

Spoon the mustard and dill sauce over the phyllo baskets and serve immediately.

Fish Puff Tart

SERVES 4

1 package frozen puff pastry,
   frozen
5 oz smoked haddock
5 oz cod

1 tbsp pesto sauce
2 tomatoes, sliced
1 cup goat's cheese, sliced
1 medium egg, beaten

freshly chopped parsley,
   to garnish

Preheat the oven to 425°F. On a lightly floured surface roll out the pastry into an
8 x 10-inch rectangle.

Draw a 7 x 9-inch rectangle in the center of the pastry, to form an 1-inch border. Be careful not
to cut through the pastry.

Lightly cut crisscross patterns in the border of the pastry with a knife.

Place the fish on a cutting board and, with a sharp knife, skin the cod and smoked haddock.
Cut into thin slices.

Spread the pesto evenly over the bottom of the pastry with the back of a spoon.

Arrange the fish, tomatoes, and cheese in the pastry, and brush the pastry with the
beaten egg.

Bake the tart in the preheated oven for 20–25 minutes, until the pastry is well risen,
puffed, and golden brown. Garnish with the chopped parsley and serve immediately.

Mussels with Creamy Garlic & Saffron Sauce

SERVES 4

1½ lb fresh live mussels
1¼ cups good-quality dry white wine
1 tbsp olive oil
1 shallot, peeled and finely chopped

2 garlic cloves, peeled and crushed
1 tbsp freshly chopped oregano
2 saffron strands
⅔ cup light cream

salt and freshly ground black pepper
fresh crusty bread, to serve

Clean the mussels thoroughly in plenty of cold water and remove any beards and barnacles from the shells. Discard any mussels that are open or damaged. Place in a large bowl, cover with cold water, and let stand in the refrigerator until required, if prepared earlier.

Pour the wine into a large saucepan and bring to a boil. Tip the mussels into the pan, cover, and cook, shaking the saucepan periodically for 6–8 minutes, or until the mussels have opened completely.

Discard any mussels with closed shells, then using a slotted spoon, carefully remove the remaining open mussels from the saucepan and keep them warm. Reserve the cooking liquid.

Heat the olive oil in a small skillet and cook the shallot and garlic gently for 2–3 minutes, until softened. Add the reserved cooking liquid and chopped oregano, and cook for a further 3–4 minutes. Stir in the saffron and the cream and heat through gently. Season to taste with salt and pepper. Place a few mussels in individual serving bowls and spoon over the saffron sauce. Serve immediately with plenty of fresh crusty bread.

Try this: FOR AN APPETIZER: 18   FOR DESSERT: 350

Parmesan & Garlic Lobster

SERVES 2

1 large cooked lobster
2 tbsp unsalted butter
4 garlic cloves, peeled
    and crushed

1 tbsp all-purpose flour
1¼ cups milk
1 cup Parmesan
    cheese, grated

sea salt and freshly ground
    black pepper
assorted lettuce leaves,
    to serve

Preheat the oven to 350°F, 10 minutes before cooking. Halve the lobster and crack the claws. Remove the gills, green sac behind the head, and the black vein running down the body. Place the two lobster halves in a shallow ovenproof dish.

Melt the butter in a small saucepan and gently cook the garlic for 3 minutes, until softened. Add the flour and stir over a medium heat for 1 minute. Draw the saucepan off the heat, then gradually stir in the milk, stirring until the sauce thickens. Return to the heat and cook for 2 minutes, stirring throughout until smooth and thickened. Stir in half the cheese and continue to cook for 1 minute, then season to taste with salt and pepper.

Pour the cheese sauce over the lobster halves and sprinkle with the remaining Parmesan cheese. Bake in the preheated oven for 20 minutes, or until heated through and the cheese sauce is golden brown. Serve with assorted lettuce leaves.

Try this: FOR AN APPETIZER: 50   FOR DESSERT: 370

Roasted Monkfish
with Parma Ham

SERVES 4

1½ lb monkfish tail
sea salt and freshly
    ground black pepper
4 bay leaves
4 slices fontina cheese,
    rind removed

8 slices Parma ham
    or prosciutto
8 oz angel hair pasta
4 tbsp butter
the zest and juice of 1 lemon
sprigs of fresh cilantro,

to garnish

To serve:
chargrilled zucchini
chargrilled tomatoes

Preheat the oven to 400°F, 15 minutes before cooking. Discard any skin from the monkfish tail and cut away and discard the central bone. Cut the fish into four equal-sized pieces and season to taste with salt and pepper. Lay a bay leaf on each fillet, along with a slice of cheese.

Wrap each fillet with two slices of the Parma ham, so that the fish is covered completely. Tuck the ends of the Parma ham in and secure with a toothpick.

Lightly oil a baking sheet and place in the preheated oven for a few minutes. Place the fish on the preheated baking sheet, then place in the oven and cook for 12–15 minutes.

Bring a large saucepan of lightly salted water to a rapid boil, then slowly add the pasta and cook for 5 minutes, or according to package directions, until cooked but firm. Drain, reserving 2 tablespoons of the liquid. Return the pasta to the saucepan and add the reserved liquid, butter, and lemon zest and juice. Toss until the pasta is well coated and glistening.

Twirl the pasta into small nests on four warmed serving plates and top with the monkfish parcels. Garnish with sprigs of cilantro and serve with chargrilled zucchini and tomatoes.

Try this: FOR AN APPETIZER: 38   FOR DESSERT: 368

Pan-fried Salmon with Herb Risotto

SERVES 4

4 x 6 oz salmon fillets,
3–4 tbsp all-purpose flour
1 tsp dried mustard powder
salt and freshly ground
   black pepper
2 tbsp olive oil
3 shallots, peeled
   and chopped

1 cup arborio or risotto rice
⅔ cup dry white wine
6 cups vegetable or
   fish stock
4 tbsp butter
2 tbsp freshly
   snipped chives
2 tbsp freshly chopped dill

2 tbsp freshly chopped
   flat-leaf parsley
1 tbsp butter

To garnish:
slices of lemon
sprigs of fresh dill
tomato salad, to serve

Wipe the salmon fillets with a clean, damp cloth. Mix together the flour, mustard powder, and seasoning on a large plate and use to coat the salmon fillets and reserve.

Heat half the olive oil in a large skillet and fry the shallots for 5 minutes, until softened but not colored. Add the rice and stir for 1 minute, then slowly add the wine, bring to a boil, and boil rapidly until reduced by half.

Bring the stock to a gentle simmer, then add to the rice, one ladleful at a time. Cook, stirring frequently, until all the stock has been added and the rice is cooked but still retains a bite. Stir in the butter and freshly chopped herbs, and season to taste with salt and pepper.

Heat the remaining olive oil and the knob of butter in a large griddle pan, add the salmon fillets, and cook for 2–3 minutes on each side, or until cooked. Arrange the herb risotto on warm serving plates and top with the salmon. Garnish with slices of lemon and sprigs of dill and serve immediately with a tomato salad.

Try this: FOR AN APPETIZER: 28   FOR DESSERT: 352

Spaghetti with Smoked Salmon & Shrimp

SERVES 4

8 cups baby spinach leaves
salt and freshly ground
    black pepper
pinch freshly grated nutmeg
8 oz large shrimp in their
    shells, cooked
1 lb fresh angel hair

spaghetti
4 tbsp butter
3 medium eggs
1 tbsp freshly chopped dill,
    plus extra to garnish
4 oz smoked salmon, cut
    into strips

dill sprigs,
    to garnish
2 tbsp grated
    Parmesan cheese,
    to serve

Cook the spinach in a large pan with 1 teaspoon of water for 3–4 minutes, or until wilted. Drain thoroughly, season to taste with salt, pepper, and nutmeg, and keep warm. Remove the shells from all but 4 of the shrimp and reserve.

Bring a large pan of lightly salted water to a rapid boil. Add the pasta and cook according to the package instructions, about 3–4 minutes, or until cooked but still firm. Drain thoroughly and return to the pan. Stir in the butter and the peeled shrimp, cover, and keep warm.

Beat the eggs with the dill, season well, then stir into the spaghetti and shrimp. Return the pan to the heat briefly, just long enough to lightly scramble the eggs, then remove from the heat. Carefully mix in the smoked salmon strips and the cooked spinach. Toss gently to mix. Tip into a warmed serving dish and garnish with the reserved shrimp and dill sprigs. Serve immediately with grated Parmesan cheese.

Try this: FOR AN APPETIZER: 24 FOR DESSERT: 366

Thai Coconut Crab Curry

SERVES 4–6

1 onion
4 garlic cloves
2-inch piece fresh ginger
2 tbsp vegetable oil
2–3 tsp hot curry paste
1¾ cups coconut milk

2 large cleaned crabs, white
　and dark meat separated
2 lemon grass stalks, peeled
　and crushed
6 green onions, trimmed
　and chopped

2 tbsp freshly shredded
　Thai basil or mint,
　plus extra, to garnish
freshly boiled rice,
　to serve

Peel the onion and chop finely. Peel the garlic cloves, then either crush or finely chop. Peel the ginger and either grate coarsely or cut into thin shreds. Reserve.

Heat a wok or large skillet and add the oil; when hot, add the onion, garlic, and ginger, and stir-fry for 2 minutes, or until the onion begins to soften. Stir in the curry paste and stir-fry for 1 minute.

Stir the coconut milk into the vegetable mixture with the dark crabmeat. Add the lemon grass, then bring the mixture slowly to a boil, stirring frequently.

Add the green onions and simmer gently for 15 minutes or until the sauce has thickened. Remove and discard the lemon grass stalks.

Add the white crabmeat and the shredded basil or mint and stir gently for 1–2 minutes or until heated through and piping hot. Try to prevent the crabmeat from breaking up.

Spoon the curry over boiled rice on warmed individual plates, sprinkle with basil or mint leaves, and serve immediately.

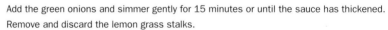

Try this: FOR AN APPETIZER: 20   FOR DESSERT: 356

Farfalle with Smoked Trout in a Dill & Vodka Sauce

SERVES 4

14 oz farfalle
5 oz smoked trout
2 tsp lemon juice
1 cup heavy cream

2 tsp whole-grain mustard
2 tbsp freshly chopped dill
4 tbsp vodka
salt and freshly ground

black pepper
sprigs of dill, to garnish

Bring a large pan of lightly salted water to a rapid boil. Add the pasta and cook according to the package instructions, or until cooked but still firm.

Meanwhile, cut the smoked trout into thin slivers, using scissors. Sprinkle lightly with the lemon juice and reserve.

Place the cream, mustard, chopped dill, and vodka in a small pan. Season lightly with salt and pepper. Bring the contents of the pan to a boil and simmer gently for 2–3 minutes, or until slightly thickened.

Drain the cooked pasta thoroughly, then return to the pan. Add the smoked trout to the dill and vodka sauce, then pour over the pasta. Toss gently until the pasta is coated and the trout evenly mixed.

Spoon into a warmed serving dish or onto individual plates. Garnish with sprigs of dill and serve immediately.

Try this: FOR AN APPETIZER: 54   FOR DESSERT: 372

Seafood Parcels with Pappardelle & Cilantro Pesto

SERVES 4

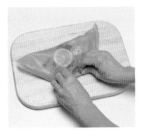

11 oz pappardelle
   or tagliatelle
8 raw large shrimp, shelled
12 raw scallops
8 oz baby squid, cleaned
   and cut into rings
4 tbsp dry white wine

4 thin slices of lemon

For the cilantro pesto:
2 cups fresh cilantro
1 garlic clove, peeled
¼ cup pine nuts, toasted
1 tsp lemon juice

5 tbsp olive oil
1 tbsp grated
   Parmesan cheese
salt and freshly ground
   black pepper

Preheat the oven to 350˚F, 10 minutes before cooking. To make the pesto, blend the cilantro, garlic, pine nuts, and lemon juice with 1 tablespoon of the olive oil to a smooth paste in a food processor. With the motor running slowly, add the remaining oil. Stir the Parmesan cheese into the pesto and season to taste with salt and pepper.

Bring a pan of lightly salted water to a rapid boil. Add the pasta and cook for 3 minutes only. Drain thoroughly, return to the pan and spoon over two-thirds of the pesto. Toss to coat.

Cut out four circles, about 12 inches in diameter, from nonstick baking parchment. Spoon the pasta onto one-half of each circle. Top each pile of pasta with 2 shrimp, 3 scallops and a few squid rings. Spoon 1 tablespoon of wine over each serving, then drizzle with the remaining cilantro pesto and top with a slice of lemon.

Close the parcels by folding over the other half of the paper to make a semicircle, then turn and twist the edges of the paper to secure.

Place the parcels on a baking sheet and bake in the preheated oven for 15 minutes, or until cooked. Serve the parcels immediately, allowing each person to open their own.

Try this: FOR AN APPETIZER: 32   FOR DESSERT: 360

Chinese Steamed Sea Bass with Black Beans

SERVES 4

2½ lb sea bass, cleaned with head and tail left on
1–2 tbsp Chinese rice wine or dry sherry
1½ tbsp peanut oil
2–3 tbsp fermented black beans, rinsed and drained
1 garlic clove, peeled and finely chopped
½-inch piece fresh ginger, peeled and finely chopped
4 green onions, trimmed and thinly sliced diagonally
2–3 tbsp soy sauce
½ cup fish or chicken stock
1–2 tbsp sweet Chinese chili sauce, or to taste
2 tsp sesame oil
sprigs of fresh cilantro, to garnish

Using a sharp knife, cut 3–4 deep diagonal slashes along both sides of the fish. Sprinkle the Chinese rice wine or sherry inside and over the fish and gently rub into the skin on both sides.

Take a heatproof plate large enough to fit into a large wok or skillet and brush with a little of the peanut oil. Place the fish on the plate, curving the fish along the inside edge of the dish, then let stand for 20 minutes.

Place a wire rack or inverted ramekin in the wok and pour in enough water to come about 1 inch up the side. Bring to a boil over a high heat. Carefully place the plate with the fish on the rack or ramekin, cover, and steam for 12–15 minutes, or until the fish is tender and the flesh is opaque when pierced with a knife near the bone.

Remove the plate with the fish from the wok and keep warm. Remove the rack or ramekin from the wok and pour off the water. Return the wok to the heat, add the remaining peanut oil, and swirl to coat the bottom and side. Add the black beans, garlic, and ginger and stir-fry for 1 minute.

Add the green onions, soy sauce, fish or chicken stock, and boil for 1 minute. Stir in the chili sauce and sesame oil, then pour the sauce over the cooked fish. Garnish with cilantro sprigs and serve immediately.

Try this: FOR AN APPETIZER: 30 FOR DESSERT: 376

Salmon & Spaghetti
in a Creamy Egg Sauce

SERVES 4

3 medium eggs
1 tbsp freshly
   chopped parsley
1 tbsp freshly chopped dill
6 tbsp freshly grated
   Parmesan cheese

6 tbsp freshly
   grated pecorino or
   Parmesan cheese
2 tbsp dry white wine
freshly ground black pepper
14 oz spaghetti

12 oz salmon fillet, skinned
2 tbsp butter
1 tsp olive oil
flat-leaf parsley sprigs,
   to garnish

Beat the eggs in a bowl with the parsley, dill, half of the Parmesan and pecorino cheeses, and the white wine. Season to taste with freshly ground black pepper and reserve.

Bring a large pan of lightly salted water to a rapid boil. Add the spaghetti and cook according to the package instructions, or until cooked but still firm.

Meanwhile, cut the salmon into bite-sized pieces. Melt the butter in a large skillet with the oil and cook the salmon pieces for 3–4 minutes, or until opaque.

Drain the spaghetti thoroughly, return to the pan, and immediately add the egg mixture. Remove from the heat and toss well; the eggs will cook in the heat of the spaghetti to make a creamy sauce.

Stir in the remaining cheeses and the cooked pieces of salmon and toss again. Tip into a warmed serving bowl or onto individual plates. Garnish with sprigs of flat-leaf parsley and serve immediately.

Try this: FOR AN APPETIZER: 60 FOR DESSERT: 364

Penne with Vodka & Caviar

SERVES 4

14 oz penne	and finely chopped	and chopped
2 tbsp butter	½ cup vodka	4½ tbsp caviar
4–6 green onions, trimmed	1 cup heavy cream	salt and freshly ground
and thinly sliced	1–2 ripe plum tomatoes,	black pepper
1 garlic clove, peeled	skinned, deseeded	

Bring a large pan of lightly salted water to a rapid boil. Add the penne and cook according to the package instructions, or until cooked but still firm. Drain thoroughly and reserve.

Heat the butter in a large skillet or wok, add the green onions, and stir-fry for 1 minute. Stir in the garlic and cook for a further 1 minute. Pour the vodka into the pan; it will bubble and steam. Cook until the vodka is reduced by about half, then add the heavy cream and return to a boil. Simmer gently for 2–3 minutes, or until the sauce has thickened slightly.

Stir in the tomatoes, then stir in all but 1 tablespoon of the caviar and season to taste with salt and pepper. Add the penne and toss lightly to coat. Cook for 1 minute, or until heated through. Divide the mixture among four warmed pasta bowls and garnish with the reserved caviar. Serve immediately.

Try this: FOR AN APPETIZER: 52   FOR DESSERT: 378

Scallops & Shrimp
Braised in Lemon Grass

SERVES 4-6

1 lb large raw shrimp,
 peeled with tails left on
12 oz scallops
2 red chile peppers,
 deseeded and
 coarsely chopped
2 garlic cloves, peeled and

 coarsely chopped
4 shallots, peeled
1 tbsp shrimp paste
2 tbsp freshly chopped
 cilantro
1¾ cups coconut milk
2–3 lemon grass stalks,

 outer leaves discarded
 and crushed
2 tbsp Thai fish sauce
1 tbsp sugar
freshly steamed basmati
 rice, to serve

Rinse the shrimp and scallops and pat dry with a paper towel. Using a sharp knife, remove the black vein along the back of the shrimp. Reserve.

Place the chile peppers, garlic, shallots, shrimp paste, and 1 tablespoon of the chopped cilantro in a food processor. Add 1 tablespoon of the coconut milk and 2 tablespoons of water, and blend to form a thick paste. Reserve the chili paste.

Pour the remaining coconut milk with 3 tablespoons of water into a large wok or skillet, add the lemon grass, and bring to a boil. Simmer over a medium heat for 10 minutes, or until reduced slightly.

Stir the chili paste, fish sauce, and sugar into the coconut milk, and continue to simmer for 2 minutes, stirring occasionally.

Add the prepared shrimp and scallops and simmer gently, for 3 minutes, stirring occasionally, or until cooked and the shrimp are pink and the scallops are opaque.

Remove the lemon grass and stir in the remaining chopped cilantro. Serve immediately spooned over freshly steamed basmati rice.

Try this: FOR AN APPETIZER: 48   FOR DESSERT: 352

Salmon Teriyaki with Noodles & Crispy Greens

SERVES 4

12 oz salmon fillet
3 tbsp Japanese soy sauce
3 tbsp mirin or sweet sherry
3 tbsp sake
1 tbsp freshly grated ginger
15 green onions

peanut oil for deep-frying
pinch of salt
½ tsp granulated sugar
4 oz cellophane noodles

To garnish:
1 tbsp freshly chopped dill
sprigs of fresh dill
zest of ½ lemon

Cut the salmon into paper-thin slices and place in a shallow dish. Mix together the soy sauce, mirin or sherry, sake, and the ginger. Pour over the salmon, cover, and let marinate for 15–30 minutes. Remove and discard the thick stalks from the green onions. Lay several leaves on top of each other, roll up tightly, then shred finely.

Pour in enough oil to cover about 2 inches of the wok. Deep-fry the green onions in batches for about 1 minute each until crisp. Remove and drain on a paper towel. Transfer to a serving dish, sprinkle with salt and sugar, and toss together.

Place the noodles in a bowl and pour over warm water to cover. Let soak for 15–20 minutes until soft, then drain. With scissors cut into 6 inch lengths.

Preheat the broiler. Remove the salmon slices from the marinade, reserving the marinade for later, and arrange them in a single layer on a baking sheet. Broil for about 2 minutes, until lightly cooked, without turning. When the oil in the wok is cool enough, tip most of it away, leaving about 1 tablespoon behind. Heat until hot, then add the noodles and the reserved marinade and stir-fry for 3–4 minutes. Tip the noodles into a large warmed serving bowl and arrange the salmon slices on top, garnished with chopped dill, sprigs of fresh dill, and lemon zest. Scatter with a little of the crispy green onions and serve the rest separately.

Try this: FOR AN APPETIZER: 36 FOR DESSERT: 358

Gnocchi & Parma Ham Bake

SERVES 4

3 tbsp olive oil
1 red onion, peeled
  and sliced
2 garlic cloves, peeled
3 plum tomatoes, skinned
  and quartered
2 tbsp sun-dried tomato paste

1 cup mascarpone cheese
salt and freshly
  ground pepper
1 tbsp freshly
  chopped tarragon
11 oz fresh gnocchi
1 cup Cheddar or Parmesan

  cheese, grated
½ cup fresh white bread
  crumbs
2 oz Parma ham, sliced
10 pitted green olives, halved
sprigs of flat-leaf parsley,
  to garnish

Heat the oven to 350˚F, 10 minutes before cooking. Heat 2 tablespoons of the olive oil in a large skillet and cook the onion and garlic for 5 minutes, or until softened. Stir in the tomatoes, sun-dried tomato paste, and mascarpone cheese. Season to taste with salt and pepper. Add half the tarragon. Bring to a boil, then lower the heat immediately and simmer for 5 minutes.

Meanwhile, bring 7 cups of water to a boil in a large pan. Add the remaining olive oil and a good pinch of salt. Add the gnocchi and cook for 1–2 minutes, or until they rise to the surface.

Drain the gnocchi thoroughly and transfer to a large ovenproof dish. Add the tomato sauce and toss gently to coat the pasta. Combine the Cheddar or Parmesan cheese with the bread crumbs and remaining tarragon, and scatter over the pasta mixture. Top with the Parma ham and olives and season again.

Cook in the preheated oven for 20–25 minutes, or until golden and bubbling. Serve immediately, garnished with parsley sprigs.

Try this: FOR AN APPETIZER: 24 FOR DESSERT: 374

Pork with Tofu

SERVES 4

1 lb smoked firm tofu
2 tbsp peanut oil
3 garlic cloves, peeled
  and crushed
1-inch piece fresh ginger,
  peeled and finely chopped
12 oz fresh ground pork

1 tbsp chill powder
1 tsp sugar
2 tbsp Chinese rice wine
1 tbsp dark soy sauce
1 tbsp light soy sauce
2 tbsp yellow bean sauce
1 tsp Szechuan peppercorns

⅛ cup chicken stock

green onions, trimmed
  and finely sliced,
  to garnish
fried rice, to serve

Cut the tofu into ½ inch cubes and place in a sieve to drain. Place the tofu on a paper towel to dry thoroughly for another 10 minutes.

Heat the wok and add the peanut oil; when hot, add the garlic and ginger. Stir-fry for a few seconds to flavor the oil, but not to color the vegetables. Add the ground pork and stir-fry for 3 minutes, or until the pork is sealed and there are no lumps in the meat.

Add all the remaining ingredients except for the tofu. Bring the mixture to a boil, then reduce the heat to low. Add the tofu and mix it in gently, taking care not to break up the tofu chunks but ensuring an even mixture of ingredients. Simmer, uncovered, for 15 minutes, or until the tofu is tender. Turn into a warmed serving dish, garnish with sliced green onions, and serve immediately with fried rice.

Apple-tossed Pork

SERVES 4

12 oz pork fillet
2 tbsp all-purpose flour
salt and black pepper
1½ tbsp sunflower oil
1 tbsp unsalted butter

2 dessert apples, peeled,
   cored, and thinly sliced
2 tsp Dijon mustard
1 tbsp freshly chopped sage
2 tbsp Calvados brandy

4 tbsp crème fraîche
   or sour cream
fresh sage leaves, to garnish
freshly cooked green beans,
   to serve

Trim away any visible fat from the pork fillet, then cut across into ½-inch thick slices. Season the flour, then add the pork slices a few at a time and toss until lightly coated.

Heat a wok, then add the oil and heat. Stir-fry the meat in two batches over a fairly high heat until well browned. Remove from the wok and reserve.

Melt the butter in the wok, add the apple slices, and cook, stirring all the time, for 1 minute. Stir in the mustard, chopped sage, Calvados brandy, and crème fraîche. Bring to a boil, stirring.

Return the pork and any juices to the wok and cook over a gentle heat for 1–2 minutes, or until the meat has warmed though, the apples are just tender, and the sauce is bubbling. Spoon onto warmed plates, garnish with fresh sage leaves, and serve immediately with freshly cooked green beans.

Try this: FOR AN APPETIZER: 40   FOR DESSERT: 362

Lamb with Black Cherry Sauce

SERVES 4

1¼ lb lamb fillet
2 tbsp light soy sauce
1 tsp Chinese five
    spice powder
4 tbsp fresh orange juice
½ cup black cherry jam

⅔ cup red wine
¼ cup fresh
    black cherries
1 tbsp peanut oil
1 tbsp freshly chopped
    cilantro, to garnish

To serve:
cooked frozen peas
freshly cooked noodles

Remove the skin and any fat from the lamb fillet and cut into thin slices. Place in a shallow dish. Mix together the soy sauce, Chinese five spice powder, and orange juice, and pour over the meat. Cover and let stand in the refrigerator for at least 30 minutes.

Meanwhile, blend the jam and the wine together, pour into a small saucepan, and bring to a boil. Simmer gently for 10 minutes until slightly thickened. Remove the pits from the cherries, using a cherry pitter if possible to keep them whole.

Drain the lamb when ready to cook. Heat the wok and add the oil, when hot, stir-fry the slices of lamb for 3–5 minutes, or until just slightly pink inside or cooked to personal preference.

Spoon the lamb into a warm serving dish and serve immediately with a little of the cherry sauce drizzled over. Garnish with the chopped cilantro and the whole cherries and serve immediately with peas, freshly cooked noodles, and the remaining sauce.

Try this: FOR AN APPETIZER: 62   FOR DESSERT: 366

Veal Escalopes with Marsala Sauce

SERVES 6

6 x 4 oz veal escalopes
lemon juice
salt and freshly ground
   black pepper
6 sage leaves
6 slices prosciutto
2 tbsp olive oil

2 tbsp butter
1 onion, peeled and sliced
1 garlic clove, peeled
   and chopped
2 tbsp Marsala wine
4 tbsp heavy cream
2 tbsp freshly

chopped parsley
sage leaves, to garnish
selection of freshly
   cooked vegetables,
   to serve

Place the veal escalopes between sheets of plastic wrap, and using a mallet or rolling pin, pound lightly to flatten out thinly to about ¼ inch thickness. Remove the plastic wrap and sprinkle the veal escalopes with lemon juice, salt, and black pepper.

Place a sage leaf in the center of each escalope. Top with a slice of prosciutto, making sure it just fits, then roll up the escalopes, enclosing the prosciutto and sage leaves. Secure each escalope with a toothpick.

Heat the olive oil and butter in a large nonstick skillet and fry the onions for 5 minutes, or until softened. Add the garlic and rolled escalopes and cook for about 8 minutes, turning occasionally, until the escalopes are browned all over.

Add the Marsala wine and cream to the skillet and bring to a boil, cover, and simmer for 10 minutes, or until the veal is tender. Season to taste, then sprinkle with the parsley. Discard the toothpicks and serve immediately with a selection of freshly cooked vegetables.

Try this: FOR AN APPETIZER: 64   FOR DESSERT: 372

Fettuccine with Calves' Liver & Brandy

SERVES 4

1 lb calves' liver, trimmed and thinly sliced	1 tsp paprika	⅔ cup heavy cream
½ cup all-purpose flour	4 tbsp butter	12 oz fresh fettuccine
salt and freshly ground black pepper	1½ tbsp olive oil	fresh thyme sprigs, to garnish
	2 tbsp Calvados brandy	
	⅔ cup apple juice	

Season the flour with the salt, black pepper, and paprika, then toss the liver in the flour until well coated.

Melt half the butter and 1 tablespoon of the olive oil in a large skillet and fry the liver in batches for 1 minute, or until just browned but still slightly pink inside. Remove using a slotted spoon and place in a warmed dish.

Add the remaining butter to the skillet, stir in 1 tablespoon of the seasoned flour, and cook for 1 minute. Pour in the brandy and apple juice, and cook over a high heat for 30 seconds. Stir the cream into the sauce and simmer for 1 minute to thicken slightly, then season to taste. Return the liver to the skillet and heat through.

Bring a large pan of lightly salted water to a rapid boil. Add the fettuccine and cook according to the package instructions, about 3–4 minutes, or until cooked but still firm.

Drain the fettuccine thoroughly, return to the pan, and toss in the remaining olive oil. Divide among 4 warmed plates and spoon the liver and sauce over the pasta. Garnish with thyme sprigs and serve immediately.

Try this: FOR AN APPETIZER: 28   FOR DESSERT: 354

Pan-fried Beef with Creamy Mushrooms

SERVES 4

8–12 medium shallots, peeled	4 plum tomatoes	4 tbsp heavy cream
2 garlic cloves, peeled	1¾ cups mushrooms	
2 tbsp olive oil	3 tbsp brandy	To serve:
4 medallions of beef	⅔ cup red wine	baby new potatoes
	salt and black pepper	freshly cooked green beans

Cut the shallots in half, then chop the garlic. Heat the oil in a large skillet and cook the shallots for about 8 minutes, stirring occasionally, until almost softened. Add the garlic and beef, and cook for 8–10 minutes, turning once during cooking until the meat is browned all over. Using a slotted spoon, transfer the beef to a plate and keep warm.

Rinse the tomatoes and cut into eighths, then clean the mushrooms and slice. Add to the skillet and cook for 5 minutes, stirring frequently until the mushrooms have softened.

Pour in the brandy and heat through. Remove the pan off the heat and carefully ignite. Allow the flames to subside. Pour in the wine, return to the heat, and bring to a boil. Boil until reduced by one-third. Remove the pan off the heat, season to taste with salt and pepper, add the cream, and stir.

Arrange the beef on serving plates and spoon over the sauce. Serve with baby new potatoes and a few green beans.

Try this: FOR AN APPETIZER: 56   FOR DESSERT: 350

Brandied Beef

SERVES 4

1 lb sirloin steak
2 tsp dark soy sauce
1 tsp dark brown sugar
salt and freshly ground
     black pepper
1 small fennel bulb

1 red bell pepper
1 orange
2 tbsp sunflower oil
1 tbsp unsalted butter
3 cups tiny button
     mushrooms

5 tbsp beef stock
3 tbsp brandy
orange wedges, to garnish
freshly cooked rice or
     noodles, to serve

Trim any fat from the steak and cut across the grain into thin strips. Place in a shallow bowl with the soy sauce, sugar, and a little salt and pepper. Mix well and let marinate while preparing the vegetables.

Trim the fennel and slice as thinly as possible, from the stems down through the root. Quarter, deseed, and thinly slice the red pepper. Thinly pare the rind from about half the orange and cut into fine matchsticks. Squeeze out the juice.

Heat the oil and butter in a wok, add the beef, and stir-fry for 2 minutes, until brown and tender. Remove with a slotted spoon and reserve.

Add the fennel, bell pepper, and mushrooms to the wok, and stir-fry for 3–4 minutes, or until softened. Add the orange zest and juice and the stock, and cook for 2 minutes, until the sauce is reduced slightly. Return the beef to the wok and stir-fry for 30 seconds to heat through.

Heat the brandy in a small saucepan or ladle, then ignite and pour over the vegetables and meat. Gently shake the wok occasionally until the flames subside. Garnish with a few orange wedges and serve immediately with rice or noodles.

Potato–stuffed Roast Poussin

SERVES 4

4 spring chicken poussins
salt and freshly ground
   black pepper
1 lemon, cut into quarters
3 medium floury potatoes
   (about 1 lb), peeled and
   cut into 1½-inch pieces

1 tbsp freshly chopped
   thyme or rosemary
3–4 tbsp olive oil
4 garlic cloves, unpeeled
   and lightly smashed
8 slices streaky bacon
   or Parma ham

½ cup white wine
2 green onions, trimmed
   and thinly sliced
2 tbsp heavy cream
   or crème fraîche
lemon wedges,
   to garnish

Preheat the oven to 425°F. Place a roasting pan in the oven to heat. Rinse the poussin cavities and pat dry with a paper towel. Season the cavities with salt and pepper and a squeeze of lemon. Push a lemon quarter into each cavity.

Put the potatoes in a saucepan of lightly salted water and bring to a boil. Reduce the heat to low and simmer until just tender; do not overcook. Drain and cool slightly. Sprinkle the chopped herbs over the potatoes and drizzle with 2–3 tablespoons of the oil. Spoon half the seasoned potatoes into the poussin cavities; do not pack too tightly. Rub each poussin with a little more oil and season with pepper. Carefully spoon 1 tablespoon of oil into the hot roasting pan and arrange the poussins in the pan. Spoon the remaining potatoes around the edge. Sprinkle over the garlic.

Roast the poussins in the preheated oven for 30 minutes, or until the skin is golden and beginning to crisp. Carefully lay the bacon slices over the breast of each poussin and continue to roast for 15–20 minutes, until crisp and the poussins are cooked through. Transfer the poussins and potatoes to a serving platter and cover loosely with foil. Skim off the fat from the juices. Place the pan over a medium heat, and add the wine and green onions. Cook briefly, scraping the bits from the bottom of the pan. Whisk in the cream or crème fraîche and bubble for 1 minute, or until thickened. Garnish the poussins with lemon wedges, and serve with the creamy gravy.

Try this: FOR AN APPETIZER: 46   FOR DESSERT: 370

Chicken with Porcini Mushrooms & Cream

SERVES 4

2 tbsp olive oil
4 boneless chicken breasts,
    preferably free range
2 garlic cloves, peeled
    and crushed
⅔ cup dry vermouth or dry

white wine
salt and freshly ground
    black pepper
2 tbsp butter
6½ cups porcini or wild
    mushrooms, thickly sliced

1 tbsp freshly
    chopped oregano
sprigs of fresh basil,
    to garnish (optional)
freshly cooked rice,
    to serve

Heat the olive oil in a large, heavy-based skillet, then add the chicken breasts, skin-side down, and cook for about 10 minutes, or until they are well browned. Remove the chicken breasts and reserve. Add the garlic, stir into the juices, and cook for 1 minute.

Pour the vermouth or white wine into the skillet and season to taste with salt and pepper. Return the chicken to the skillet. Bring to a boil, reduce the heat to low, and simmer for about 20 minutes, or until tender.

In another large skillet, heat the butter and add the sliced porcini or wild mushrooms. Stir-fry for about 5 minutes, or until the mushrooms are golden and tender.

Add the porcini or wild mushrooms and any juices to the chicken. Season to taste, then add the chopped oregano. Stir together gently and cook for 1 minute longer. Transfer to a large serving plate and garnish with sprigs of fresh basil, if desired. Serve immediately with rice.

Try this: FOR AN APPETIZER: 42   FOR DESSERT: 360

Crispy Chicken Noodles

SERVES 4

1 medium egg white
2 tsp cornstarch
salt and freshly ground
    white pepper
8 oz boneless and
    skinless chicken
    breast, diced

8 oz medium Chinese
    egg noodles
1 cup peanut oil
2 tbsp Chinese
    rice wine
2 tbsp oyster sauce
1 tbsp light soy sauce

1¼ cups chicken stock
1 tbsp cornstarch

To garnish:
green onion curls
toasted cashew nuts

Mix the egg white with the cornstarch in a bowl, season to taste with salt and pepper, then add the chicken and stir to coat. Chill in the refrigerator for 20 minutes. Blanch the noodles for 2 minutes in a large saucepan of boiling salted water and drain.

Heat a wok or large skillet and add 2 tablespoons of the peanut oil. When hot, spread the noodles evenly over the surface, reduce the heat to low, and cook for about 5 minutes, or until browned on one side. Gently turn over, adding extra oil if necessary, and cook until both sides are browned. Reserve and keep warm.

Drain the chicken. Wipe the wok clean, reheat, and add the remaining peanut oil. When hot, add the chicken and stir-fry for 2 minutes. Using a slotted spoon, remove and drain on a paper towel. Keep warm.

Wipe the wok clean, reheat, and pour in the Chinese rice wine, oyster sauce, soy sauce, and chicken stock, and season lightly. Bring to a boil. Blend the cornstarch with 2 tablespoons of water to make a paste and stir into the wok. Cook, stirring, until the sauce has thickened. Cook for a further minute. Tip the noodles onto warmed plates, top with the crispy chicken pieces, and drizzle over the sauce. Garnish with spring onion curls (see page 48) and sprinkle with toasted cashew nuts. Serve immediately.

Herb–baked Chicken with Tagliatelle

SERVES 4

¾ cup fresh white bread
   crumbs
3 tbsp olive oil
1 tsp dried oregano
2 tbsp sun-dried
   tomato paste

salt and freshly ground
   black pepper
4 x 5 oz boneless and
   skinless chicken breasts,
2 x 14-oz can plum tomatoes
4 tbsp freshly chopped basil

2 tbsp dry white wine
12 oz tagliatelle
fresh basil sprigs,
   to garnish

Preheat the oven to 400°F, 15 minutes before cooking. Mix together the bread crumbs, 1 tablespoon of the olive oil, the oregano, and tomato paste. Season to taste with salt and pepper. Place the chicken breasts well apart in a roasting pan and coat with the bread crumb mixture.

Mix the plum tomatoes with the chopped basil and white wine. Season to taste, then spoon evenly round the chicken.

Drizzle the remaining olive oil over the chicken breasts and cook in the preheated oven for 20–30 minutes, or until the chicken is golden and the juices run clear when a skewer is inserted into the flesh.

Meanwhile, bring a large pan of lightly salted water to a rapid boil. Add the pasta and cook according to the package instructions, or until cooked but still firm.

Drain the pasta thoroughly and transfer to warmed serving plates. Arrange the chicken breasts on top of the pasta and spoon over the sauce. Garnish with sprigs of basil and serve immediately.

Try this: FOR AN APPETIZER: 52 FOR DESSERT: 356

Parma Ham–wrapped Chicken with Ribbon Pasta

SERVES 4

4 boneless and skinless
   chicken breasts
salt and black pepper
12 slices Parma ham
   or prosciutto
2 tbsp olive oil
12 oz ribbon pasta

1 garlic clove, peeled and
   chopped
1 bunch green onions,
   trimmed and
   diagonally sliced
14-oz can chopped tomatoes
juice of 1 lemon

⅔ cup crème fraîche or
   heavy cream
3 tbsp freshly
   chopped parsley
pinch of sugar
freshly grated Parmesan
   cheese, to garnish

Cut each chicken breast into three pieces and season well with salt and pepper. Wrap each chicken piece in a slice of Parma ham to enclose completely, securing if necessary with either fine twine or toothpicks.

Heat the oil in a large skillet and cook the chicken, turning occasionally, for 12–15 minutes, or until thoroughly cooked. Remove from the skillet with a slotted spoon and reserve.

Meanwhile, bring a large pan of lightly salted water to a rapid boil. Add the pasta and cook according to the package instructions, or until cooked but still firm.

Add the garlic and green onions to the skillet and cook, stirring occasionally, for 2 minutes, or until softened. Stir in the tomatoes, lemon juice, and crème fraîche. Bring to a boil, lower the heat, and simmer, covered, for 3 minutes. Stir in the parsley and sugar, season to taste, then return the chicken to the skillet and heat for 2–3 minutes, or until piping hot.

Drain the pasta thoroughly and mix in the chopped parsley, then spoon onto a warmed serving dish or individual plates. Arrange the chicken and sauce over the pasta. Garnish and serve immediately.

Try this: FOR AN APPETIZER: 44   FOR DESSERT: 378

Szechuan Sesame Chicken

SERVES 4

1 medium egg white
pinch of salt
2 tsp cornstarch
1 lb boneless, skinless
   chicken breast, cut into
   3-inch strips
1¼ cups peanut oil

1 tbsp sesame seeds
2 tsp dark soy sauce
2 tsp cider vinegar
2 tsp chili bean sauce
2 tsp sesame oil
2 tsp sugar
1 tbsp Chinese rice wine

1 tsp whole Szechuan
   peppercorns, roasted
2 tbsp green onion, trimmed
   and finely chopped
mixed salad, to serve

Beat the egg white with a pinch of salt and the cornstarch, pour into a shallow dish, and add the chicken strips. Turn to coat, cover with plastic wrap, and let stand in the refrigerator for 20 minutes.

Heat a wok and add the peanut oil; when hot, add the chicken pieces and stir-fry for 2 minutes or until the chicken turns white. Using a slotted spoon, remove the chicken, and drain on a paper towel. Pour off the oil and reserve 1 tablespoon of the oil. Wipe the wok clean.

Reheat the wok, add 1 tablespoon of the peanut oil with the sesame seeds, and stir-fry for 30 seconds, or until golden. Stir in the dark soy sauce, cider vinegar, chili bean sauce, sesame oil, sugar, Chinese rice wine, Szechuan peppercorns, and the green onions. Bring to a boil.

Return the chicken to the wok and stir-fry for 2 minutes, making sure that the chicken is coated evenly with the sauce and sesame seeds. Turn into a warmed serving dish and serve immediately with a mixed salad.

Try this: FOR AN APPETIZER: 30   FOR DESSERT: 364

Creamy Chicken Stroganoff

SERVES 4

1 lb skinless chicken
   breast fillets
4 tbsp dry sherry
4 dried porcini mushrooms
2 tbsp sunflower oil
2 tbsp unsalted butter
1 onion, peeled
   and sliced

3 cups button mushrooms,
   cleaned and sliced
1 tbsp paprika
1 tsp freshly chopped thyme
½ cup chicken stock
⅔ cup crème fraîche
salt and freshly ground
   black pepper

sprigs of fresh thyme,
   to garnish

To serve:
crème fraîche or sour cream
freshly cooked rice
   or egg noodles

Cut the chicken into finger-length strips and reserve. Gently warm the sherry in a small saucepan and remove from the heat. Add the porcini mushrooms and let soak while preparing the rest of the stir-fry.

Heat a wok and add 1½ tablespoons of the oil; when hot, add the chicken and stir-fry over a high heat for 3–4 minutes, or until lightly browned. Remove from the wok and reserve.

Heat the remaining oil and butter in the wok and gently cook the onion for 5 minutes. Add the button mushrooms and stir-fry for a further 5 minutes, or until tender. Sprinkle in the paprika and thyme and cook for 30 seconds.

Add the porcini mushrooms with their soaking liquid, then stir in the stock and return the chicken to the wok. Cook for 1–2 minutes, or until the chicken is cooked through and tender.

Stir in the crème fraîche and heat until piping hot. Season to taste with salt and pepper. Garnish with sprigs of fresh thyme and serve immediately with a spoonful of crème fraîche and rice or egg noodles.

Try this: FOR AN APPETIZER: 56 FOR DESSERT: 354

Garlic Mushrooms with
Crispy Bacon & Chicken Liver Sauté

SERVES 4

4 large field mushrooms
3 tbsp butter, melted
  and cooled
2 garlic cloves, peeled
  and crushed
1 tbsp sunflower oil
3 slices smoked streaky

bacon, derinded
  and chopped
4 shallots, peeled and
  thinly sliced
1 lb chicken livers, halved
2 tbsp marsala or
  sweet sherry

4 tbsp chicken or
  vegetable stock
6 tbsp heavy cream
2 tsp freshly chopped thyme
salt and freshly ground
  black pepper

Remove the stalks from the mushrooms and roughly chop. Mix together 2 tablespoons of the butter and garlic and brush over both sides of the mushroom caps. Place on the rack of a broiler pan.

Heat a wok and add the oil; when hot, add the bacon and stir-fry for 2–3 minutes, or until crispy. Remove and reserve. Add the remaining butter to the wok and stir-fry the shallots and chopped mushroom stalks for 4–5 minutes, until they are softened.

Add the chicken livers and cook for 3–4 minutes, or until well browned on the outside but still pink and tender inside. Pour in the marsala or sherry and the stock. Simmer for 1 minute, then stir in the cream, thyme, salt and pepper, and half the bacon. Cook for about 30 seconds to heat through.

While the livers are frying, cook the mushroom caps under a hot broiler for 3–4 minutes each side, until tender.

Place the mushrooms on warmed serving plates, allowing one per person. Spoon the chicken livers over and around the mushrooms. Scatter with the remaining bacon and serve immediately.

Try this: FOR AN APPETIZER: 36   FOR DESSERT: 372

Sesame–coated Turkey with Mango Tabbouleh

SERVES 4

3 turkey breast fillets
(about 1 lb), skinned
4 tbsp all-purpose flour
4 tbsp sesame seeds
salt and freshly ground
black pepper
1 medium egg, lightly beaten
2 tbsp sunflower oil

For the mango tabbouleh:
1 cup bulgar wheat
2 tbsp olive oil
juice of ½ lemon
6 green onions,
trimmed and
finely chopped
1 red chile pepper, deseeded

and finely chopped
1 ripe mango, peeled,
pitted, and diced
3 tbsp freshly
chopped cilantro
1 tbsp freshly chopped
mint leaves

Cut the turkey across the grain into strips. Mix together the flour, sesame seeds, and salt and pepper. Dip the turkey strips in the beaten egg, then in the sesame seed mixture to coat. Chill in the refrigerator until ready to cook.

For the tabbouleh, put the bulgar in a large bowl and pour over plenty of boiling water. Cover the bowl with a plate and let soak for 20 minutes.

Whisk together the olive oil and lemon juice in a large bowl. Stir in the green onions, chile pepper, mango, cilantro, and mint. Drain the bulgar and squeeze out any excess moisture with your hands, then add to the bowl, season to taste with salt and pepper, and mix well.

Heat a wok and add the oil; when hot, stir-fry the sesame-coated turkey strips in two batches for 4–5 minutes, or until golden, crispy, and cooked through. Divide the turkey strips between individual serving plates and serve immediately with the tabbouleh.

Try this: FOR AN APPETIZER: 32   FOR DESSERT: 380

Duck in Black Bean Sauce

SERVES 4

1 lb duck breast, skinned	2 green onions	shredded green onions,
1 tbsp light soy sauce	2 tbsp Chinese preserved	to garnish
1 tbsp Chinese rice wine	black beans	freshly cooked noodles,
or dry sherry	1 tbsp peanut or vegetable	to serve
1-inch piece fresh ginger	oil	
3 garlic cloves	⅔ cup chicken stock	

Using a sharp knife, trim the duck breasts, removing any fat. Slice thickly and place in a shallow dish. Mix together the soy sauce and Chinese rice wine or sherry and pour over the duck. Let marinate for 1 hour in the refrigerator, then drain and discard the marinade.

Peel the ginger and chop finely. Peel the garlic cloves and either chop finely or crush. Trim the root from the green onions, discard the outer leaves, and chop. Finely chop the black beans.

Heat a wok or large skillet, add the oil, and when hot, add the ginger, garlic, green onions, and black beans, and stir-fry for 30 seconds. Add the drained duck and stir-fry for 3–5 minutes, or until the duck is browned.

Add the chicken stock to the wok, bring to a boil, then reduce the heat and simmer for 5 minutes, or until the duck is cooked and the sauce is reduced and thickened. Remove from the heat. Tip onto a bed of freshly cooked noodles, garnish with green onion shreds and serve immediately.

Try this: FOR AN APPETIZER: 62   FOR DESSERT: 374

Hoisin Duck & Greens Stir Fry

SERVES 4

12 oz duck breasts,
    skinned and cut into strips
1 medium egg white, beaten
½ tsp salt
1 tsp sesame oil
2 tsp cornstarch
2 tbsp peanut oil

2 tbsp freshly grated ginger
¼ cup bamboo shoots
½ cup fine green beans,
    trimmed
⅓ cup pak choi, chopped
2 tbsp hoisin sauce
1 tsp Chinese rice wine

or dry sherry
zest and juice of ½ orange
strips of orange zest,
    to garnish
freshly steamed egg
    noodles, to serve

Place the duck strips in a shallow dish, then add the egg white, salt, sesame oil, and cornstarch. Stir lightly until the duck is coated in the mixture. Cover and chill in the refrigerator for 20 minutes.

Heat the wok until hot and add the oil. Remove the wok from the heat and add the duck, stirring continuously to prevent the duck from sticking to the wok. Add the ginger and stir-fry for 2 minutes. Add the bamboo shoots, the green beans, and the pak choi, and stir-fry for 1–2 minutes, until wilted.

Mix together the hoisin sauce, the Chinese rice wine or sherry, and the orange zest and juice. Pour into the wok and stir to coat the duck and vegetables. Stir-fry for 1–2 minutes, or until the duck and vegetables are tender. Garnish with the strips of orange zest and serve immediately with freshly steamed egg noodles.

Try this: FOR AN APPETIZER: 20 FOR DESSERT: 360

Honey–glazed Duck in Kumquat Sauce

SERVES 4

4 duck breast fillets
1 tbsp light soy sauce
1 tsp sesame oil
1 tbsp clear honey
3 tbsp brandy
1 tbsp sunflower oil

2 tbsp granulated sugar
1 tbsp white wine vinegar
⅔ cup orange juice
5 kumquats,
    thinly sliced
2 tsp cornstarch

salt and freshly ground
    black pepper
fresh watercress,
    to garnish
basmati and wild rice,
    to serve

Thinly slice the duck breasts and put in a shallow bowl. Mix together the soy sauce, sesame oil, honey, and 1 tablespoon of brandy. Pour over the duck, stir well, cover, and marinate in the refrigerator for at least 1 hour.

Heat a wok until hot, add the sunflower oil, and swirl it round to coat the sides. Drain the duck, reserving the marinade, and stir-fry over a high heat for 2–3 minutes, or until browned. Remove from the wok; reserve.

Wipe the wok clean with a paper towel. Add the sugar, vinegar, and 1 tablespoon of water. Gently heat until the sugar dissolves, then boil until a rich golden color. Pour in the orange juice, then the remaining brandy. Stir in the kumquat slices and simmer for 5 minutes.

Blend the cornstarch with 1 tablespoon of cold water to make a paste. Add to the wok and simmer for 2–3 minutes, stirring until thickened. Return the duck to the wok and cook gently for 1–2 minutes, or until warmed through. Season to taste with salt and pepper. Spoon onto warmed plates and garnish with fresh watercress leaves. Serve immediately with freshly cooked basmati and wild rice.

Try this: FOR AN APPETIZER: 42   FOR DESSERT: 362

Stir-fried Greens

SERVES 4

½ head Chinese cabbage
  (about 1 lb)
1½ cups pak choi
1 cup broccoli florets
1 tbsp sesame seeds
1 tbsp peanut oil
1 tbsp fresh ginger, peeled

  and finely chopped
3 garlic cloves, peeled
  and finely chopped
2 red chile peppers,
  deseeded and split in half
¼ cup chicken stock
2 tbsp Chinese rice wine

1 tbsp dark soy sauce
1 tsp light soy sauce
2 tsp black bean sauce
freshly ground black pepper
2 tsp sugar
1 tsp sesame oil

Separate the Chinese cabbage and pak choi leaves, wash well, and cut into 1-inch strips. Separate the broccoli into small florets. Heat a wok or large skillet, add the sesame seeds, and stir-fry for 30 seconds or until browned.

Add the oil to the wok and when hot, add the ginger, garlic, and chile peppers, and stir-fry for 30 seconds. Add the broccoli and stir-fry for 1 minute. Add the Chinese cabbage and pak choi and stir-fry for a further 1 minute.

Pour the chicken stock and Chinese rice wine into the wok with the soy and black bean sauces. Season to taste with pepper and add the sugar. Reduce the heat and simmer for 6–8 minutes, or until the vegetables are tender but still firm to the bite. Tip into a warmed serving dish, removing the chile peppers if preferred. Drizzle with the sesame oil and serve immediately.

Vegetables in Coconut Milk with Rice Noodles

SERVES 4

2 tbsp sunflower oil
2 garlic cloves, peeled and
   finely chopped
2 red bell peppers, deseeded
   and cut into thin strips
1-inch piece of fresh ginger,

peeled and cut into thin
   strips
2½ cups coconut milk
16 baby sweet corn
2 tsp cornstarch
2 medium ripe but still

firm avocados
1 small romaine lettuce,
   cut into thick strips
freshly cooked rice noodles,
   to serve

Heat a wok or large skillet, add the oil and when hot, add the chopped garlic, sliced bell peppers, and ginger. Cook for 30 seconds, then cover and cook gently for 10 minutes, or until the peppers are soft.

Pour in the coconut milk and bring to a boil. Stir in the baby sweet corn, cover, and simmer for 5 minutes. Blend the cornstarch with 2 teaspoons of water, pour into the wok, and cook, stirring, for 2 minutes or until thickened slightly.

Cut the avocados in half, peel, remove the stone, and slice. Add to the wok with the lettuce strips and stir until well mixed and heated through. Serve immediately on a bed of rice noodles.

Try this: FOR AN APPETIZER: 26   FOR DESSERT: 368

Tomato & Zucchini Herb Tart

SERVES 4

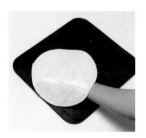

4 tbsp olive oil
1 onion, peeled and
    finely chopped
3 garlic cloves, peeled
and crushed
1 14-oz package puff pastry,

thawed if frozen
1 small egg, beaten
2 tbsp freshly
    chopped rosemary
2 tbsp freshly
    chopped parsley

1½ cups rindless fresh
    soft goat's cheese
4 ripe plum tomatoes, sliced
1 medium zucchini, trimmed
    and sliced
thyme sprigs, to garnish

Preheat the oven to 450°F. Heat 2 tablespoons of the oil in a large skillet. Fry the onion and garlic for about 4 minutes until softened and reserve.

Roll out the pastry on a lightly floured surface, and cut out a 12-inch circle. Brush the pastry with a little beaten egg, then prick all over with a fork. Transfer onto a dampened baking sheet and bake in the preheated oven for 10 minutes.

Turn the pastry over and brush with a little more egg. Bake for 5 more minutes, then remove from the oven.

Mix together the onion, garlic, and herbs with the goat's cheese and spread over the pastry. Arrange the tomatoes and zucchini over the goat's cheese and drizzle with the remaining oil.

Bake for 20–25 minutes, or until the pastry is golden brown and the topping bubbling. Garnish with the thyme sprigs and serve immediately.

Try this: FOR AN APPETIZER: 54   FOR DESSERT: 370

Desserts

Creamy Pudding with Mixed Berry Compote

SERVES 6

1¼ cups heavy cream
1 cup ricotta cheese
¼ cup granulated sugar
4 oz white chocolate, broken

into pieces
2⅓ cups mixed berries, such
as strawberries,
blueberries, and

raspberries
2 tbsp Cointreau

Whip the cream until soft peaks form. Fold in the ricotta cheese and half the sugar.

Place the chocolate in a bowl set over a saucepan of simmering water. Stir until melted. Remove from the heat and let cool, stirring occasionally. Stir into the cheese mixture until well blended.

Spoon the mixture into six individual dessert molds and level the surface of each pudding with the back of a spoon. Place in the freezer and freeze for 4 hours.

Place the fruits and the remaining sugar in a pan and heat gently, stirring occasionally until the sugar has dissolved and the juices are just beginning to run. Stir in the Cointreau to taste.

Dip the dessert molds in hot water for 30 seconds and invert onto six serving plates. Spoon the fruit compote over the puddings and serve immediately.

Try this: FOR AN APPETIZER: 54 FOR THE MAIN MEAL: 200

Lemon Surprise

SERVES 4

6 tbsp margarine
¾ cup granulated sugar
3 medium eggs, separated
¾ cup all-purpose flour

2 cups semi-skimmed milk
juice of 2 lemons
juice of 1 orange
2 tsp confectioners' sugar

lemon twists, to decorate
sliced strawberries,
    to serve

Preheat the oven to 375°F. Lightly oil a deep ovenproof dish.

Beat together the margarine and sugar until pale and fluffy. Add the egg yolks, one at a time, with 1 tablespoon of the flour, and beat well after each addition. Once added, stir in the remaining flour.

Stir in the milk, 4 tablespoons of the lemon juice, and 3 tablespoons of the orange juice. Whisk the egg whites until stiff, and fold into the egg mixture with a metal spoon or rubber spatula until well combined. Pour into the prepared dish.

Stand the dish in a roasting pan and pour in just enough boiling water to come halfway up the sides of the dish.

Bake in the preheated oven for 45 minutes, until well risen and spongy to the touch.

Remove the pudding from the oven and sprinkle with the confectioners' sugar. Decorate with the lemon twists and serve immediately with the strawberries.

Coffee & Peach Cream

SERVES 4

4 peaches
¼ cup granulated sugar
2 tbsp coffee
    extract

10-oz package vanilla
    pudding
1 cup plain yogurt

To decorate:
peach slices
sprigs of mint
heavy cream, whipped

Cut the peaches in half and remove the stones. Place the peaches in a large bowl, cover with boiling water, and let stand for 2–3 minutes.

Drain the peaches, then carefully remove the skin.

Place the granulated sugar in a saucepan and add a ¼ cup of water. Bring the sugar mixture to a boil, stirring occasionally, until the sugar has dissolved. Boil rapidly for about 2 minutes.

Add the peaches and coffee extract to the pan. Remove from the heat and allow the peach mixture to cool.

Meanwhile, make the vanilla pudding, following the package directions and let cool. Mix together the yogurt and vanilla pudding until well combined.

Divide the peaches between four glass dishes. Spoon over the vanilla pudding mixture then top with the remaining peach mixture.

Chill for 30 minutes and then serve, decorated with peach slices, mint sprigs, and a little heavy cream.

Try this: FOR AN APPETIZER: 24   FOR THE MAIN MEAL: 106

Orange–flavored Chocolate Mousse

SERVES 6

6 oz orange-flavored
   chocolate
2 cups vanilla pudding,
   already prepared

2 cups heavy cream
12 tomatillos,
   to decorate
cookies, to serve

Break the chocolate into segments and place in a bowl set over a saucepan of simmering water. Heat until the chocolate melts, stirring occasionally. Remove the bowl from the heat and let the melted chocolate cool slightly.

Place the vanilla pudding in a bowl and fold the melted chocolate into it, using a metal spoon or rubber spatula. Stir well until completely combined.

Pour the cream into a small bowl and whip until the cream forms soft peaks. Using a metal spoon or rubber spatula, fold in most of the whipped cream into the chocolate mixture.

Spoon into six tall glasses and carefully top with the remaining cream.

Let the desserts chill in the refrigerator for at least 1 hour, but preferably overnight.

Peel back the skins from the tomatillos to form petal shapes and use to decorate the chocolate desserts. Serve with the cookies.

Try this: FOR AN APPETIZER: 38   FOR THE MAIN MEAL: 146

Crunchy Rhubarb Crumble

SERVES 6

1 cup all-purpose flour
4 tbsp softened butter
⅔ cup rolled oats

¼ cup light brown sugar
1 tbsp sesame seeds
½ tsp ground cinnamon

1 lb fresh rhubarb
¼ cup granulated sugar
custard or cream, to serve

Preheat the oven to 350°F. Place the flour in a large bowl and cut the butter into cubes. Add to the flour and rub in with the fingertips until the mixture looks like fine bread crumbs, or blend for a few seconds in a food processor.

Stir in the rolled oats, brown sugar, sesame seeds, and cinnamon. Mix well and reserve.

Prepare the rhubarb by removing the thick ends of the stalks and cut diagonally into 1-inch chunks. Wash thoroughly and pat dry with a clean kitchen towel. Place the rhubarb in a small ovenproof dish.

Sprinkle the granulated sugar over the rhubarb and top with the reserved crumble mixture. Level the top of the crumble so that all the fruit is well covered and press down firmly. If you prefer, sprinkle the top with a little extra granulated sugar.

Place on a baking sheet and bake in the preheated oven for 40–50 minutes, or until the fruit is soft and the topping is golden brown. Sprinkle the dessert with some more granulated sugar and serve hot with custard or cream.

Try this: FOR AN APPETIZER: 64   FOR THE MAIN MEAL: 82

Crème Brûlée with Sugared Raspberries

SERVES 6

2½ cups heavy cream
4 medium egg yolks
6 tbsp granulated sugar

½ tsp vanilla extract
2 tbsp light brown sugar
1½ cups fresh raspberries

Preheat the oven to 300°F. Pour the cream into a bowl and place over a saucepan of gently simmering water. Heat gently but do not allow to boil.

Meanwhile, whisk together the egg yolks, 4 tablespoons of the granulated sugar, and the vanilla extract. When the cream is warm, pour it over the egg mixture, briskly whisking until it is mixed completely. Pour into 6 individual ramekin dishes and place in a roasting pan.

Fill the pan with sufficient water to come halfway up the sides of the dishes. Bake in the preheated oven for about 1 hour, or until the puddings are set. To test if set, carefully insert a round bladed knife into the center. If the knife comes out clean, they are set.

Remove the puddings from the roasting pan and let cool. Chill in the refrigerator, preferably overnight.

Sprinkle the light brown sugar over the top of each dish and place the puddings under a preheated hot broiler. When the sugar has caramelized and turned deep brown, remove from the heat and cool. Chill the puddings in the refrigerator for 2–3 hours before serving.

Toss the raspberries in the remaining granulated sugar and sprinkle over the top of each dish. Serve with a little extra cream if you want.

Chocolate Sponge Cake with Fudge Sauce

SERVES 4

6 tbsp butter
6 tbsp granulated sugar
2 oz plain chocolate, melted
½ cup all-purpose flour
4½ tbsp cocoa powder
1 large egg
1 tbsp confectioners' sugar,
    to dust
crème fraîche or whipped
    heavy cream, to serve

For the fudge sauce:
¼ cup light brown sugar
1 tbsp cocoa powder
⅓ cup pecans,
    roughly chopped
2 tbsp granulated sugar
1¼ cups hot, strong black
    coffee

Preheat the oven to 325°F. Oil a small, shallow heatproof dish.

Cream the butter and the sugar together in a large bowl until light and fluffy. Stir in the melted chocolate, flour, cocoa powder, and egg, and mix together. Turn the mixture into the prepared dish and level the surface.

To make the fudge sauce, blend the brown sugar, cocoa powder, and pecans together, and sprinkle evenly over the top of the chocolate mixture.

Stir the granulated sugar into the hot black coffee until it has dissolved. Carefully pour the coffee over the top of the dessert.

Bake in the preheated oven for 50–60 minutes, until the top is firm to touch. There will now be a rich sauce underneath the sponge.

Remove from the oven, dust with confectioners' sugar and serve hot with crème fraîche or whipped cream.

Try this: FOR AN APPETIZER: 60   FOR THE MAIN MEAL: 110

Golden Castle Pudding

SERVES 4–6

½ cup (1 stick) butter
½ cup granulated sugar
a few drops vanilla extract

2 medium eggs, beaten
1 cup all-purpose flour
4 tbsp corn syrup

crème fraîche or whipped
heavy cream, to serve

Preheat the oven to 350°F. Lightly oil 4–6 individual custard cups and place a small circle of lightly oiled nonstick baking or wax paper in the bottom of each one.

Place the butter and granulated sugar in a large bowl, then beat together until the mixture is pale and creamy. Stir in the vanilla extract and gradually add the beaten eggs, a little at a time. Add a tablespoon of flour after each addition of egg and beat well.

When the mixture is smooth, add the remaining flour, and fold in gently. Add a tablespoon of water and mix to form a soft mixture that will drop easily off a spoon.

Spoon enough mixture into each custard cup to come halfway up, allowing enough space for the puddings to rise. Place on a baking sheet and bake in the preheated oven for about 25 minutes, until firm and golden brown.

Let the puddings stand for 5 minutes. Discard the paper circle and turn out onto individual serving plates.

Warm the corn syrup in a small saucepan and pour a little over each pudding. Serve hot with the crème fraîche or whipped heavy cream.

Try this: FOR AN APPETIZER: 36   FOR THE MAIN MEAL: 130

Cherry Batter Pudding

SERVES 4

1 lb fresh cherries (or
    15-oz can pitted cherries)
½ cup all-purpose flour
pinch of salt

3 tbsp granulated sugar
2 medium eggs
1¼ cups milk
3 tbsp butter

1 tbsp rum
extra granulated sugar,
    to dredge
fresh cream, to serve

Preheat the oven to 425˚F. Lightly oil a 1-quart shallow baking dish.

Rinse the cherries, drain well, and remove the pits (using a cherry pitter if possible).
If using canned cherries, drain well, discard the juice, and place in the prepared dish.

Sift the flour and salt into a large bowl. Stir in 2 tablespoons of the granulated sugar and
make a well in the center. Beat the eggs, then pour into the well of the dry ingredients.

Warm the milk and slowly pour into the well, beating throughout and gradually pulling in the
flour from the sides of the bowl. Continue until a smooth batter has formed.

Melt the butter in a small saucepan over a low heat, then stir into the batter with the rum.
Reserve for 15 minutes, then beat again until smooth and easy to pour.

Pour into the prepared baking dish and bake in the preheated oven for 30–35 minutes,
or until golden brown and set.

Remove the dessert from the oven, sprinkle with the remaining sugar, and serve hot with
plenty of fresh cream.

Try this: FOR AN APPETIZER: 24 FOR THE MAIN MEAL: 154

Vanilla & Lemon Panna Cotta with Raspberry Sauce

SERVES 6

3¾ cups heavy cream	5 tbsp milk	sugar, to taste
1 vanilla pod, split	1 ½ tsp unflavored gelatin	1 tbsp lemon juice
7 tbsp granulated sugar	3½ cups raspberries	extra lemon zest,
zest of 1 lemon	3–4 tbsp confectioners'	to decorate

Put the cream, vanilla pod, and sugar into a saucepan. Bring to a boil, then simmer for 10 minutes until slightly reduced, stirring to prevent scalding. Remove from the heat, stir in the lemon zest, and remove the vanilla pod. Meanwhile, sprinkle gelatin over the milk and allow to soak for 5 minutes. Add the gelatin mixture to the saucepan and stir well until dissolved.

Pour the cream mixture into six ramekins and let stand in the refrigerator for 4 hours, or until set.

Meanwhile, put 1½ cups of the raspberries in a food processor with the confectioners' sugar and lemon juice. Blend to a puree, then pass the mixture through a sieve. Fold in the remaining raspberries with a metal spoon or rubber spatula, and chill in the refrigerator until ready to serve.

To serve, dip each of the ramekins into hot water for a few seconds, then turn out onto six individual serving plates. Spoon some of the raspberry sauce over and around the panna cotta, decorate with extra lemon zest, and serve.

Try this: FOR AN APPETIZER: 40   FOR THE MAIN MEAL: 140

Ricotta Cheesecake with Strawberry Coulis

SERVES 6-8

8 Graham crackers
3½ oz candied peel, chopped
5 tbsp butter, melted
⅔ cup crème fraîche or
   heavy cream

1 cup ricotta cheese
7 tbsp granulated sugar
1 vanilla pod, seeds only
2 large eggs
1½ cups strawberries

2–4 tbsp granulated sugar,
   to taste
zest and juice of 1 orange

Preheat the oven to 325°F. Line an 8-inch springform pan with baking parchment. Place the crackers into a food processor together with the peel. Blend until the crackers are crushed and the peel is chopped. Add 4 tablespoons of the melted butter and process until mixed. Tip into the pan and spread evenly over the bottom. Press firmly into place and reserve.

Blend together the crème fraîche, ricotta cheese, sugar, vanilla seeds, and eggs in a food processor. With the motor running, add the remaining melted butter and blend for a few seconds. Pour the mixture over the bottom. Transfer to the preheated oven and cook for about 1 hour, until set and risen around the edges, but slightly wobbly in the center. Switch off the oven and let cool in it. Chill in the refrigerator for at least 8 hours, or preferably overnight.

Wash and drain the strawberries. Hull the fruit and remove any soft spots. Put into the food processor along with 2 tablespoons of the sugar and the orange juice and zest. Blend until smooth. Add the remaining sugar to taste. Pass through a sieve to remove seeds and chill in the refrigerator until needed.

Cut the cheesecake into wedges, spoon over some of the strawberry coulis and serve.

Try this: FOR AN APPETIZER: 50   FOR THE MAIN MEAL: 188

Mixed Berries Semifreddo

SERVES 6–8

1¾ cups raspberries
1 cup blueberries
1 cup red currants
¼ cup confectioners' sugar

juice of 1 lemon
1 vanilla pod, split
¼ cup granulated sugar
4 large eggs, separated

2¼ cups heavy cream
pinch of salt
fresh red currants,
    to decorate

Wash and hull or remove stalks from the fruit, as necessary, then put them into a food processor or blender with the confectioners' sugar and lemon juice. Blend to a puree, pour into a jug, and chill in the refrigerator, until needed.

Remove the seeds from the vanilla pod by opening the pod and scraping with the back of a knife. Add the seeds to the granulated sugar and whisk with the egg yolks until pale and thick.

In another bowl, whip the cream until soft peaks form. Do not overwhip. In a third bowl, whip the egg whites with the salt until stiff peaks form.

Using a large metal spoon—to avoid knocking any air from the mixture—fold together the fruit puree, egg yolk mixture, the cream, and egg whites. Transfer the mixture to a round, shallow, freezer box, cover with the lid, and put into the freezer until almost frozen. If the mixture freezes solid, thaw in the refrigerator until semifrozen. Turn out the semifrozen mixture, cut into wedges, and serve decorated with a few fresh red currants. If the mixture thaws completely, eat immediately and do not refreeze.

Try this: FOR AN APPETIZER: 62   FOR THE MAIN MEAL: 168

Baked Stuffed Amaretti Peaches

SERVES 4

4 ripe peaches
grated zest and juice
  of 1 lemon
8 Amaretti cookies
⅔ cup chopped blanched

almonds, toasted
½ cup pine nuts, toasted
3 tbsp brown sugar
4 tbsp butter
1 medium egg yolk

2 tsp clear honey
crème fraîche or plain
  yogurt, to serve

Preheat the oven to 350°F. Halve the peaches and remove the pits. Take a thin slice from the bottom of each peach half so that it will sit flat on the baking sheet. Dip the peach halves in lemon juice and arrange on a baking sheet.

Crush the Amaretti cookies lightly and put into a large bowl. Add the almonds, pine nuts, sugar, lemon zest, and butter. Work with the fingertips until the mixture resembles coarse bread crumbs. Add the egg yolk and mix well until the mixture is just binding.

Divide the Amaretti-and-nut mixture between the peach halves, pressing down lightly. Bake in the preheated oven for 15 minutes, or until the peaches are tender and the filling is golden. Remove from the oven and drizzle with the honey.

Place two peach halves on each serving plate and spoon over a little crème fraîche or yogurt, then serve.

Try this: FOR AN APPETIZER: 42   FOR THE MAIN MEAL: 204

Zabaglione with Rum-soaked Raisin Compote

SERVES 6

2 tbsp raisins	3 tbsp Marsala wine	⅔ cup heavy cream, lightly
1 strip thinly pared	3 medium egg yolks	whipped
lemon zest	3 tbsp granulated sugar	crisp cookies,
½ tsp ground cinnamon	½ cup dry white wine	to serve

Put the raisins in a small bowl with the lemon zest and ground cinnamon. Pour over the Marsala wine to cover and let macerate for at least one hour. When the raisins are plump, lift out of the Marsala wine and reserve the raisins and wine; discard the lemon zest.

In a large heatproof bowl, mix together the egg yolks and sugar. Add the white wine and Marsala wine and stir well to combine. Put the bowl over a saucepan of simmering water, ensuring that the bottom of the bowl does not touch the water. Whisk constantly until the mixture doubles in bulk.

Remove from the heat and continue whisking for about 5 minutes until the mixture has cooled slightly. Fold in the raisins and then immediately fold in the whipped cream. Spoon into dessert glasses or goblets and serve with crisp cookies.

Try this: FOR AN APPETIZER: 48   FOR THE MAIN MEAL: 136

Tiramisu

SERVES 4

2 cups mascarpone cheese
2 tbsp confectioners' sugar, sifted
⅔ cup strong coffee, chilled
1¼ cups heavy cream

3 tbsp coffee liqueur
16 lady fingers
2 oz plain chocolate, grated or made into small curls
cocoa powder, for dusting

assorted mixed berries, to serve

Lightly oil and line a 2-pound loaf pan with a piece of plastic wrap. Put the mascarpone cheese and confectioners' sugar into a large bowl and using a rubber spatula, beat until smooth. Stir in 2 tablespoons of chilled coffee and mix thoroughly.

Whip the cream with 1 tablespoon of the coffee liqueur until just thickened. Stir a spoonful of the whipped cream into the mascarpone mixture, then fold in the rest. Spoon half of the the mascarpone mixture into the prepared loaf pan and smooth the top.

Put the remaining coffee and coffee liqueur into a shallow dish just bigger than the lady fingers. Using half of the fingers, dip one side of each finger into the coffee mixture, then arrange on top of the mascarpone mixture in a single layer. Spoon the rest of the mascarpone mixture over the fingers and smooth the top.

Dip the remaining fingers in the coffee mixture and arrange on top of the mascarpone mixture. Drizzle with any remaining coffee mixture. Cover with plastic wrap and chill in the refrigerator for 4 hours.

Carefully turn the tiramisu out onto a large serving plate and sprinkle with the grated chocolate or chocolate curls. Dust with cocoa powder, cut into slices, and serve with a few mixed berries.

Try this: FOR AN APPETIZER: 64   FOR THE MAIN MEAL: 98

Stir-fried Bananas & Peaches with Rum Butterscotch Sauce

SERVES 4

2 medium-firm bananas
1 tbsp granulated sugar
2 tsp lime juice
4 firm, ripe peaches
    or nectarines

1 tbsp sunflower oil

For the rum butterscotch
    sauce:
4 tbsp unsalted butter

1 cup light brown sugar
1¼ cups heavy cream
2 tbsp dark rum

Peel the bananas and cut into 1-inch diagonal slices. Place in a bowl and sprinkle with the granulated sugar and lime juice, and stir until lightly coated. Reserve.

Place the peaches or nectarines in a large bowl and pour over boiling water to cover. Let stand for 30 seconds, then plunge them into cold water and peel off their skins. Cut each one into 8 thick slices, discarding the stone.

Heat a wok, add the oil, and swirl it round the wok to coat the sides. Add the fruit and cook for 3–4 minutes, shaking the wok and gently turning the fruit until lightly browned. Spoon the fruit into a warmed serving bowl and clean the wok with a paper towel.

Add the butter and sugar to the wok and stir continuously over a low heat until the sugar has dissolved. Remove from the heat and let cool for 2–3 minutes.

Stir the cream and rum into the sugar syrup and return to the heat. Bring to a boil and simmer for 2 minutes, stirring continuously until smooth. Let cool slightly for 2–3 minutes, then serve warm with the stir-fried peaches and bananas.

Try this: FOR AN APPETIZER: 44   FOR THE MAIN MEAL: 160

Index